KU-450-297

Contents

		page
Introduction		v
Chapter 1	Growing Up Black	1
Chapter 2	The Store	2
Chapter 3	Life in Stamps	9
Chapter 4	Momma	13
Chapter 5	A New Family	19
Chapter 6	Mr. Freeman	27
Chapter 7	Return to Stamps	38
Chapter 8	Two Women	40
Chapter 9	Friends	49
Chapter 10	Graduation	58
Chapter 11	California	63
Chapter 12	Education	71
Chapter 13	A Vacation	75
Chapter 14	San Francisco	87
Chapter 15	Maturity	93
Activities		101

I Know Why
the Caged Bird Sings

MAYA ANGELOU

Level 6

Retold by Jacqueline Kehl
Series Editors: Andy Hopkins and Jocelyn Potter

Pearson Education Limited
Edinburgh Gate, Harlow,
Essex CM20 2JE, England
and Associated Companies throughout the world.

ISBN-13: 978-0-582-50524-7
ISBN-10: 0-582-50524-0

First published in the USA by Random House 1969
Published in the UK by Virago Press 1984
This edition first published 2002

5 7 9 10 8 6 4

Typeset by Ferdinand Pageworks, London
Set in 11/14pt Bembo
Reproduction by Spectrum Colour, Ipswich
Printed in China
SWTC/04

Published by Pearson Education Limited in association with
Penguin Books Ltd, both companies being subsidiaries of Pearson Plc

For a complete list of titles available in the Penguin Readers series please write to your local
Pearson Education office or contact: Penguin Readers Marketing Department,
Pearson Education, Edinburgh Gate, Harlow, Essex, CM20 2JE.

Introduction

In Stamps the segregation was so complete that most Black children didn't really, absolutely know what whites looked like. We knew only that they were different, to be feared, and in that fear was included the hostility of the powerless against the powerful, the poor against the rich, the worker against the employer, and the poorly dressed against the well dressed.

At the age of three, Maya and her brother were sent to live with their grandmother in Stamps, Arkansas. What was life like for a poor Black girl growing up in the segregated American South in the 1930s and 1940s? What kinds of prejudice did she experience, and how did they affect her?

Between the ages of three and sixteen, Maya also lived in St. Louis and California. She moved often, and knew good times as well as bad, kindness and great cruelty. Despite shockingly tragic childhood experiences, she managed to keep her sense of hope and achievement. This is Maya's story.

Maya Angelou (born in 1928) is a well-known Black American writer. *I Know Why the Caged Bird Sings* (1969) is the first of five books she wrote about her life. The others are *Gather Together in My Name* (1974), *Singin' and Swingin' and Gettin' Merry Like Christmas* (1976), *The Heart of a Woman* (1981), and *All God's Children Need Traveling Shoes* (1988). She has also written novels, plays, poetry, movies, short stories, children's books, and magazine articles. Ms. Angelou is a life-time professor of American Studies at Wake Forest University in North Carolina. She also lectures throughout the U.S. and the world.

Chapter 1   Growing Up Black

"What you looking at me for?
I didn't come to stay ..."

I hadn't forgotten the next line, but I couldn't make myself remember. Other things were more important. Whether I could remember the rest of the poem or not didn't matter. The truth of the statement was like a wet handkerchief crushed in my fists. The sooner they accepted it, the quicker I could let my hands open and the air would cool them.

"What you looking at me for ...?"

The children's section of the Colored Methodist Episcopal Church was laughing at my well-known forgetfulness.

The dress I wore was light purple. As I'd watched Momma make it, putting fancy stitching on the waist, I knew that when I put it on I'd look like one of the sweet little white girls who were everyone's dream of what was right with the world. Hanging softly over the black Singer sewing machine, it looked like magic. When people saw me wearing it, they were going to run up to me and say, "Marguerite [sometimes it was 'dear Marguerite'], forgive us, please, we didn't know who you were," and I would answer generously, "No, you couldn't have known. Of course I forgive you."

Just thinking about it made me feel heavenly for days. But Easter's early morning sun had shown the dress to be a plain ugly one made from a white woman's faded purple throwaway. It was long like an old lady's dress, but it didn't hide my legs. The faded color made my skin look dirty like mud, and everyone in church was looking at my thin legs.

1

Wouldn't they be surprised when one day I woke out of my black ugly dream, and my real hair, which was long and blonde, would take the place of the kinky mass that Momma wouldn't let me straighten? When they saw my light-blue eyes, they would understand why I had never picked up a Southern accent, or spoken the language like they did, and why I had to be forced to eat pigs' tails. Because I was really white and a cruel magician had turned me into a too-big Negro girl, with kinky black hair, broad feet, and a space between her teeth that would hold a pencil.

"What you looking ..." The minister's wife leaned toward me, her long yellow face full of sorry. I held up two fingers, close to my chest, which meant that I had to go to the toilet, and walked quietly toward the back of the church. My head was up and my eyes were open, but I didn't see anything. Before I reached the door, the sting was burning down my legs and into my Sunday socks. I tried to hold it, to squeeze it back, to keep it from spreading, but when I reached the church porch I knew I'd have to let it go. If I didn't, it would probably run right back up to my head and my poor head would burst, and all the brains and spit and tongue and eyes would roll all over the place. So I ran down into the yard and let it go. I ran, peeing and crying, not toward the toilet out back but to our house. I'd get a whipping for it, and the nasty children would have a reason to laugh at me. I laughed anyway, partly for the sweet release; the greater joy came not only from being set free from the silly church but from the knowledge that I wouldn't die from a burst head.

If growing up is painful for the Southern Black girl, being aware of her difference is worse. It is an unnecessary insult.

Chapter 2   The Store

When I was three and Bailey four, we had arrived in the dusty

2

little town, wearing notes on our wrists which stated—"To Whom It May Concern"—that we were Marguerite and Bailey Johnson Jr.,* from Long Beach, California, on our way to Stamps, Arkansas, to Mrs. Annie Henderson.

Our parents had decided to put an end to their disastrous marriage, and Father shipped us home to his mother. The conductor on the train had been asked to take care of us, and our tickets were pinned to my brother's inside coat pocket.

I don't remember much of the trip, but after we reached the segregated southern part of the journey, things must have improved. Negro passengers, who always traveled with full lunch boxes, felt sorry for "the poor little motherless darlings" and gave us lots of cold fried chicken and potato salad.

The town reacted to us as its residents had reacted to all things new before our arrival. It regarded us for a while without curiosity but cautiously, and after we were seen to be harmless (and children) it closed in around us, as a real mother welcomes a stranger's child. Warmly, but not affectionately.

We lived with our grandmother and uncle in the back of the Store (it was always spoken of with a capital S), which she had owned for around twenty-five years.

Early in the century, Momma (we soon stopped calling her Grandmother) sold lunches to laborers in the two factories in Stamps. Her delicious meat pies and cool lemonade made her business a success. At first she went to the factories. Later she set up a stand between them and supplied the workers' needs for a few years. Then she had the Store built in the heart of the Negro area. There customers could find basic foods, a good variety of colored thread, pig food, corn for chickens, coal oil for lamps, light bulbs for the wealthy, shoestrings, balloons, and flower seeds. Anything not visible could be ordered.

* Jr.: short for Junior

3

◆

When Bailey was six and I a year younger, we could repeat the multiplication tables extraordinarily quickly. Uncle Willie used to sit, like a huge black Z (he had been crippled as a child), and listen to us. His face pulled down on the left side, and his left hand was only a little bigger than Bailey's.

Momma related countless times, and without any show of emotion, how Uncle Willie had been dropped when he was three years old by a woman who was taking care of him. She seemed to hold no anger against the baby-sitter, nor for her God who allowed the accident. She felt it necessary to explain over and over again to those who knew the story by heart that he wasn't "born that way."

In our society, where two-legged, two-armed strong Black men were able at best to earn enough for only the necessities of life, Uncle Willie was the subject of jokes of the underemployed and underpaid. He was proud and sensitive, so he couldn't pretend that he wasn't crippled; nor could he pretend that people were not disgusted by his body.

Only once in all the years of trying not to watch him, I saw him pretend to himself and others that he wasn't crippled.

Coming home from school one day, I saw a dark car in our front yard. I rushed in and found a strange man and woman drinking Dr. Pepper in the cool of the Store. I sensed a wrongness around me.

I knew it couldn't be the strangers. When I looked at Uncle Willie, I knew what was happening. He was standing erect behind the counter, not leaning forward or resting on the small shelf that had been built for him. His eyes seemed to hold me with a mixture of threats and appeal.

I dutifully greeted the strangers and my eyes wandered around looking for his walking stick. It was nowhere to be seen. He said,

4

"This . . . this . . . my niece. She's . . . just come from school. You know . . . how . . . children are . . . th-th-these days . . . they play all d-d-day at school and c-c-can't wait to get home and pl-play some more."

The people smiled, very friendly.

He added, "Go on out and pl-play, Sister."

The lady laughed and said, "Well, you know, Mr. Johnson, they say you're only a child once. Have you any children of your own?"

Before I left, I saw him lean back on the shelves of chewing tobacco. "No, ma'am . . . no ch-children and no wife." He tried a laugh. "I have an old m-m-mother and my brother's t-two children to l-look after."

I didn't mind him using us to make himself look good. In fact, I would have pretended to be his daughter if he wanted me to. Not only did I not feel any loyalty to my own father, I figured that if I had been Uncle Willy's child, I would have received much better treatment.

The couple left after a few minutes, and Uncle Willie made his way between the shelves and the counter—hand over hand. From the back of the house, I watched him move awkwardly from one side, bumping into the other, until he reached the coal-oil tank. He put his hand behind it and took his walking stick in his strong fist and shifted his weight on the wooden support. He thought he had succeeded in his pretense.

I'll never know why it was important to him that the couple would take a picture of a whole Mr. Johnson home with them. He must have tired of being a cripple, tired of the high-topped shoes and the walking stick, his uncontrollable muscles and thick tongue, and the looks of pity he suffered. For one afternoon, one part of an afternoon, he wanted to be rid of them.

I understood, and felt closer to him in that moment than ever before or since.

◆

During these years in Stamps, I met and fell in love with William Shakespeare. He was my first white love. Although I enjoyed and respected Kipling, Poe, Butler, Thackeray, and Henley, I saved my young and loyal love for Paul Lawrence Dunbar, Langston Hughes, James Weldon Johnson, and W.E.B. Du Bois's "Litany at Atlanta." But it was Shakespeare who said, "When in disgrace with fortune and men's eyes." It was a state with which I felt myself most familiar. I accepted his whiteness by telling myself that he had been dead for so long it couldn't matter to anyone anymore.

Bailey and I decided to memorize a scene from *The Merchant of Venice*, but we realized that Momma would question us about the author and that we'd have to tell her that Shakespeare was white, and it wouldn't matter to her whether he was dead or not. So we chose "The Creation" by James Weldon Johnson instead.

♦

Weighing the half-pounds of flour and putting them dust-free into the thin paper sacks was a simple kind of adventure for me. I developed an eye for measuring how full a container of flour, sugar, or corn had to be to push the scale indicator over to eight ounces or one pound. When I was absolutely accurate, our appreciative customers used to praise me: "Sister Henderson sure got some smart grandchildren." If I made a mistake in the Store's favor, the eagle-eyed women would say, "Put some more in that sack, child. Don't you try to make your profit off me."

Then I would quietly punish myself. For every bad judgment, the fine was no silver-wrapped Kisses, the sweet chocolate candy that I loved more than anything in the world, except Bailey. And maybe canned pineapples. My love of them nearly drove me mad. I dreamt of the days when I would be grown and able to buy a whole carton for myself alone.

Although the sweet golden rings sat in their cans on our

shelves all year, we only tasted them during Christmas. Momma used the juice to make almost-black fruit cakes. Then she lined heavy iron pans with the pineapple rings for rich upside-down cakes. Bailey and I received one slice each, and I carried mine around for hours, picking off small pieces of the fruit until nothing was left except the perfume on my fingers. I'd like to think that my desire for pineapples was so special that I wouldn't allow myself to steal a can (which was possible) and eat it alone out in the garden. But I'm certain that I must have considered the possibility that others would notice the smell on my fingers, and didn't dare to attempt it.

Until I was thirteen and left Arkansas for ever, the Store was my favorite place to be. Alone and empty in the mornings, it looked like an unopened present from a stranger. Opening the front doors was pulling the ribbon off an unexpected gift. The light would come in softly (we faced north), slowly moving over the shelves of canned fish, tobacco, thread. Whenever I walked into the Store in the afternoon, I sensed that it was tired. Only I could hear the slow heartbeat of its job half done. But just before bedtime, after numerous people had walked in and out, had argued over their bills, or joked about their neighbors, or just dropped in to say hello, the promise of magic mornings returned to the Store.

Momma opened boxes of crackers and we sat around the meat block at the back of the Store. I sliced onions, and Bailey opened two or even three cans of fish. That was supper. In the evening, when we were alone like that, Uncle Willie didn't stutter or shake or give any indication that he had a problem. It seemed that the peace of a day's ending was an assurance that the understanding God had with children, Negroes, and the crippled was still good.

◆

Throwing handfuls of corn to the chickens and mixing leftover food and oily dish water for the pigs were among our evening chores. Bailey and I walked down the trails to the pig yard, and standing on the fence we poured the unappealing mess down to our grateful pigs.

Late one day, as we were feeding the pigs, I heard a horse in the front yard (it really should have been called a driveway, except that there was nothing to drive into it), and ran to find out who had come riding up on a Thursday evening. The used-to-be sheriff sat on his horse in such a way that his attitude was meant to show his authority and power over even dumb animals. How much more authority he would have over Negroes. Nothing needed to be said.

From the side of the Store, Bailey and I heard him say to Momma, "Annie, tell Willie he'd better stay out of sight tonight. A crazy nigger* assaulted a white lady today. Some of the boys'll be coming over here later." Even now, I remember the sense of fear which filled my mouth with hot, dry air, and made my body light.

The "boys"? Those cement faces and eyes of hate that burned the clothes off you if they saw you standing around on the main street downtown on Saturday. Boys? It seemed that youth had never happened to them. Boys? No, men filled with the ugliness and rottenness of old hatreds.

The used-to-be sheriff was confident that my uncle and every other Black man who heard of the Klan's† planned ride would quickly go under their houses to hide with the chickens. Without waiting for Momma's thanks, he rode out of the yard, sure that things were as they should be and that he was a gentle

* nigger: an offensive word for a Negro, or Black person.

† the Klan: the Ku Klux Klan, an organization of white people who commit hate crimes against Black people.

master, saving those deserving servants from the law of the land, which he supported.

Immediately, Momma blew out the coal-oil lamps. She had a quiet talk with Uncle Willie and called Bailey and me into the Store.

We were told to take the potatoes and onions out of their containers and knock out the dividing walls that kept them apart. Then, with a fearful slowness, Uncle bent down to get into the empty space. It took for ever before he lay down flat, and then we covered him with potatoes and onions, layer upon layer. Grandmother knelt praying in the darkened Store.

It was fortunate that the "boys" didn't ride into our yard that evening and insist that Momma open the Store. They would have surely found Uncle Willie and just as surely killed him. He cried the whole night as if he had, in fact, been guilty of some awful crime.

Chapter 3   Life in Stamps

The difference between a Southern town and a Northern town must be the experiences of childhood. Heroes and enemies are first met, and values and dislikes are first learned and labeled in that early environment.

Mr. McElroy, who lived in the big house next to the Store, was very tall and broad. He was the only Negro I knew, except for the school principal and the visiting teachers, who wore matching pants and jacket. He never laughed, seldom smiled, and he liked to talk to Uncle Willie. He never went to church, which Bailey and I thought also proved he was a very courageous person. How great it would be to grow up like that, to be able to ignore religion, especially living next door to a woman like Momma.

9

I watched him with the excitement of expecting him to do anything at any time. I never tired of this, or became disappointed with him. There seemed to be an understanding between Mr. McElroy and Grandmother. This was obvious to us because he never chased us off his land. In summer's late sunshine I often sat under the tree in his yard, surrounded by the bitter smell of its fruit and the sound of flies that fed on the berries. He sat in a swing on his porch, rocking in his brown three-piece suit.

One greeting a day was all that could be expected from Mr. McElroy. After his "Good morning, child," or "Good afternoon, child," he never said a word, even if I met him again on the road in front of his house or down by the well, or ran into him behind the house, escaping in a game of hide-and-seek.

He remained a mystery in my childhood. A man who owned his land and the big many-windowed house with a porch that went all around the house. An independent Black man. A rare occurrence in Stamps.

♦

Bailey was the greatest person in my world. And the fact that he was my brother, my only brother, and I had no sisters to share him with, was such good fortune that it made me want to live a Christian life just to show God that I was grateful. I was big, elbowy, and rough, but he was small, graceful, and smooth. I was described by our friends as being brown, but he was praised for his dark black skin. His hair fell down in black curls, and my head was covered with tight, kinky curls. But he loved me.

When adults said unkind things about my features (my family's good looks were painful to me), Bailey would look at me from across the room, and I knew that it was just a matter of time before he would take revenge. He would allow the old ladies to finish wondering where my features came from, then he would ask, in a voice like cooling bacon grease, "Oh, Mrs. Coleman, how is your son? I saw him the other day, and he looked sick enough to die."

Astonished, the ladies would ask, "Die? From what? He ain't sick."

And in a voice oilier than the one before, he'd answer with no expression on his face, "From the Uglies."

I would hold my laugh, bite my tongue, and very seriously remove even the slightest smile from my face. Later, behind the house, we'd laugh and laugh.

Bailey could be sure of very few punishments for his frequent offensive behavior, because he was the pride of the Henderson–Johnson family.

His movements were carefully calculated. He was also able to find more hours in the day than I thought existed. He finished his chores and homework, read more books than I, and played games on the side of the hill with the other children. He could even pray out loud in church, and was skilled at stealing candy from the barrel that sat under the fruit counter and Uncle Willie's nose.

Of all the needs (there are none imaginary) a lonely child has, the one that must be satisfied, if there is going to be hope and a hope of wholeness, is the unshaking need for an unshakable God. My pretty Black brother was mine.

♦

In Stamps the custom was to can everything that could possibly be preserved. All the neighbors helped each other to kill pigs. The ladies of the Christian Methodist Episcopal Church helped Momma prepare the pork for sausage. They squeezed their fat arms elbow deep in the cut-up meat, mixed it, and gave a small taste to all obedient children who brought wood for the black stove. The men cut off the larger pieces of meat and laid them in the smokehouse to begin the preservation process.

11

Throughout the year, until the next frost, we took our meals from the smokehouse, the little garden close to the Store, and the shelves of canned foods. But at least twice yearly Momma would feel that as children we should have fresh meat included in our diets. We were then given money—pennies, nickels, and dimes handed to Bailey—and sent to town to buy some. Since the whites had refrigerators, their stores brought meat from Texarkana and sold it to the wealthy even in the peak of summer.

Crossing the Black area of Stamps, which to a child seemed a whole world, we were expected to stop and speak to every person we met, and Bailey felt he had to spend a few minutes playing with each friend. There was a joy in going to town with money in our pockets (Bailey's pockets were as good as my own) and plenty of time. But the pleasure left us when we reached the white part of town.

In Stamps the segregation was so complete that most Black children didn't really, absolutely know what whites looked like. We knew only that they were different, to be feared, and in that fear was included the hostility of the powerless against the powerful, the poor against the rich, the worker against the employer, and the poorly dressed against the well dressed.

I remember never believing that whites were really real. I couldn't force myself to think of them as people. People were Mrs. LaGrone, Mrs. Hendricks, Momma, Lillie B, and Louise and Rex. Whitefolks couldn't be people because their feet were too small, their skin too white, and they didn't walk on their flat feet the way people did—they walked on their heels like horses.

People were those who lived on my side of town. I didn't like them all, or, in fact, any of them very much, but they were people. These other strange pale creatures weren't considered folks. They were whitefolks.

Chapter 4   Momma

"You shall not be dirty" and "You shall not be impudent" were the two commandments of Grandmother Henderson by which we lived.

Each night in the bitterest winter we were forced to wash faces, arms, necks, legs, and feet before going to bed. We would go to the well and wash in the ice-cold, clear water, grease our legs, then walk carefully into the house. We wiped the dust from our toes and settled down for schoolwork, cornbread, milk, prayers, and bed, always in that order. Momma was famous for pulling the blankets off after we had fallen asleep to examine our feet. If they weren't clean enough for her, she took the stick (she kept one behind the door for emergencies) and woke up the offender with a few well-placed burning reminders. She made sure we learned the importance of cleanliness.

Politeness was also important. The impudent child was hated by God and a shame to its parents and could bring ruin to its house and family. All adults had to be addressed as Mister, Missus, or Miss. Everyone I knew respected these customary laws, except for the poor-white-trash children.

Some families of "poor white trash" lived on Momma's farm land behind the school. Sometimes a group of them came to the Store. They called my uncle by his first name and ordered him around the Store. He, to my shame, obeyed them.

My grandmother, too, followed their orders, except that she didn't seem like a servant because she anticipated their needs.

"Here's sugar, Miss Potter, and here's baking powder. You didn't buy baking soda last month, you'll probably be needing some."

Momma always directed her statements to the adults, but sometimes the dirty girls would answer her.

"No, Annie . . ." they said. To Momma, who owned the land

they lived on? Who forgot more than they would ever learn? "Just give us some extra crackers, and some more fish."

At least they never looked her in the face, or I never caught them doing so. Nobody with any training at all would look right in a grown person's face. It meant the person was trying to take the words out before they were formed. The dirty little children didn't do that, but they threw their orders around the Store like strikes of a whip.

When I was around ten years old, those children caused me the most painful and confusing experience I had ever had with my grandmother.

One summer morning, after I had swept the dirt yard of leaves, gum wrappers, and Vienna-sausage can labels, I swept the yellow dirt, and made half-moons carefully, so that the design was clear. Then I went behind the Store, came through the back of the house, and found Grandmother on the front porch in her big, white apron. Momma was admiring the yard, so I joined her. She didn't say anything, but I knew she liked it. She looked over toward the school principal's house and to the right at Mr. McElroy's. She was hoping one of those important people would see the design before the day's business wiped it out. Then she looked upward to the school. My head had swung with hers, so at just about the same time we saw a group of poor-white-trash kids marching over the hill and down by the side of the school.

I looked at Momma for direction. She stood straight and began to sing quietly. She didn't look at me again. When the children reached halfway down the hill, halfway to the Store, she said without turning, "Sister, go on inside."

I wanted to beg her, "Momma, don't wait for them. Come on inside with me. If they come in the Store, you go to the bedroom and let me serve them. They only frighten me if you're around. Alone, I know how to handle them." But of course I couldn't say anything, so I went in and stood behind the screen door.

Before the girls got to the porch I heard their laughter. I suppose my life-long distrust was born in those cold, slow minutes. They finally came to stand on the ground in front of Momma. One of them folded her arms, pushed out her mouth, and started to sing quietly. I realized that she was imitating my grandmother. Another said, "No, Helen, you ain't standing like her. This is it." Then she lifted her chest and folded her arms, copying that strange way of standing that was Annie Henderson. Another laughed, "No, you can't do it. Your mouth ain't pushed out enough. It's like this."

I thought about the rifle behind the door, but I knew I'd never be able to hold it straight, and our other gun was locked in the trunk, and Uncle Willie had the key on his chain. Through the screen door, I could see that the arms of Momma's apron shook with her singing. But her knees seemed to have locked as if they would never bend again.

She sang on. No louder than before, but no softer either. No slower or faster.

The girls had tired of imitating Momma and turned to other ways to make her respond. One crossed her eyes, stuck her thumbs in both sides of her mouth, and said, "Look here, Annie." Grandmother sang on, and the apron strings trembled. I wanted to throw a handful of black pepper in their faces, to scream that they were dirty, but I knew I couldn't do anything.

One of the smaller girls did a kind of dance while the others laughed at her. But the tall one, who was almost a woman, said something very quietly, which I couldn't hear. They all moved backward from the porch, still watching Momma. For an awful second I thought they were going to throw a rock at Momma, who seemed (except for the apron strings) to have turned into stone herself. But the big girl turned her back, bent down, and put her hands flat on the ground. She didn't pick up anything— she just did a handstand.

Her dirty bare feet and long legs went straight for the sky. Her dress fell down around her shoulders, and she had on no underpants. She hung like that for only a few seconds, then fell.

Momma changed her song to a religious song. I found that I was praying too. How long could Momma continue? What would they think of to do to her next? Would I be able to stay out of it? What would Momma really like me to do?

Then they were moving out of the yard, on their way to town. They nodded their heads and shook their thin behinds and turned, one at a time.

"Bye, Annie."

"Bye, Annie."

"Bye, Annie."

Momma never turned her head or unfolded her arms, but she stopped singing and said, "Bye, Miss Helen, bye, Miss Ruth, bye, Miss Eloise."

I burst. How could Momma call them Miss? The mean nasty things. Why couldn't she have come inside the sweet, cool store when we saw them coming over the hill? What did she prove? And then, if they were dirty, mean, and impudent, why did Momma have to call them Miss?

She stood there for another whole song and then opened the screen door to look down on me crying in anger. She looked until I looked up. Her face was a brown moon that shone on me. She was beautiful. Something had happened out there, which I couldn't completely understand, but I could see that she was happy. Then she bent down and touched me, and I grew quiet.

"Go wash your face, Sister." And she went behind the candy counter and sang, "Glory, glory, praise the Lord."

I threw the well water on my face and used the weekly handkerchief to blow my nose. Whatever the contest had been, I knew Momma had won.

I went back to the front yard. The footprints were easy to

sweep away. I worked for a long time on my new design. When I came back in the Store, I took Momma's hand and we both walked outside to look at the new pattern.

It was a large heart with lots of hearts growing smaller inside, and going from the outside edge to the smallest heart was an arrow. Momma said, "Sister, that's very pretty." Then she turned back to the Store and continued, "Glory, glory, praise the Lord, when I lay my burden down."

◆

People spoke of Momma as a good-looking woman, and some, who remembered her youth, said she used to be very pretty. I saw only her power and strength. She was taller than any woman in my personal world, and her hands were so large they could reach around my head from ear to ear. Her voice was soft only because she chose to keep it so. In church, when she was asked to lead the singing, the sound would pour over the listeners and fill the air.

Momma intended to teach Bailey and me to use the paths of life that she and people of her age and all the Negroes gone before had found, and found to be safe ones. She didn't agree with the idea that whitefolks could be talked to at all without risking one's life. And certainly they couldn't be spoken to impudently. In fact, even in their absence they could not be spoken of too badly unless we used the reference "They." If she had been asked and had chosen to answer the question of whether she was cowardly or not, she would have said that she believed in reality. Didn't she stand up to "them" year after year? Wasn't she the only Negro woman in Stamps referred to once as Mrs.?

Some years before Bailey and I arrived in town, a man was hunted for assaulting a white woman. In trying to escape he ran to the Store. Momma and Uncle Willie hid him behind the dresser until night, gave him supplies for an overland journey, and sent him on his way. He was, however, caught, and in court when he was questioned about his movements on the day of the crime, he replied that after he heard that he was being sought he hid in Mrs. Henderson's Store.

The judge asked that Mrs. Henderson appear in court, and when Momma arrived and said she was Mrs. Henderson, the judge and other whites in the audience laughed. The judge had really made a mistake calling a Negro woman "Mrs.," but he was from Pine Bluff and couldn't have been expected to know that a woman who owned a store in the village would also be colored. The whites laughed about the incident for a long time, and the Negroes thought it proved the worth and honor of my grandmother.

♦

People in Stamps used to say that the whites in our town were so prejudiced that a Negro couldn't buy white ice cream. Except on July Fourth. Other days he had to be satisfied with chocolate.

A curtain had been drawn between the Black community and all things white, but one could see through it enough to develop fear, admiration, and contempt for the white "things"— whitefolks' cars and white houses and their children and their women. But above all, their wealth that allowed them to waste was the most enviable. They had so many clothes that they were able to give away perfectly good dresses, faded just under the arms, to the sewing class at our school for the larger girls to practice on.

I couldn't understand whites and where they got the right to spend money so freely. Of course, I knew God was white too, but no one could have made me believe he was prejudiced. My grandmother had more money than all the poor white trash. We owned land and houses, but each day Bailey and I were reminded, "Waste not, want not."

Momma bought two rolls of cloth each year for winter and

summer clothes. She made my school dresses and handkerchiefs, Bailey's shirts and shorts, her aprons and house dresses from these. Uncle Willie was the only person in the family who wore ready-to-wear clothes all the time. Each day he wore fresh white shirts, and his special shoes cost twenty dollars. I thought Uncle Willie was sinfully proud, especially when I had to iron seven shirts.

Chapter 5   A New Family

One Christmas we received gifts from our mother and father, who lived separately in a heaven called California. We had been told that in California they could have all the oranges they could eat and the sun shone all the time. I was sure that wasn't true. I couldn't believe that our mother would laugh and eat oranges in the sunshine without her children. Until that Christmas when we received the gifts, I had been confident that they were both dead.

Then came that terrible Christmas with its awful presents when our father, with the pride I later learned was typical, sent his photograph. My gift from Mother was a tea set and a doll with blue eyes and rosy cheeks and yellow hair painted on her head. I don't know what Bailey received, but after I opened my boxes I went out to the backyard behind the tree. The day was cold. Frost was still on the bench, but I sat down and cried. I looked up and Bailey was coming toward me, wiping his eyes. He had been crying too. I didn't know if he had also told himself they were dead and had been shocked by the truth, or whether he was just feeling lonely. The gifts opened the door to questions that neither of us wanted to ask. Why did they send us away? What did we do so wrong? Why, at three and four, were we sent by train alone from Long Beach, California, to Stamps, Arkansas, with notes attached to our arms and only the conductor to look after us?

Bailey sat down beside me, and that time didn't tell me not to cry. So I cried, but we didn't talk until Momma called us back in the house.

"You children are the most ungrateful things I ever saw," she said. "You think your mother and father took all the trouble to send you these nice presents to make you go out in the cold and cry?"

Neither of us said a word. Momma continued, "Sister, I know you're tender-hearted, but Bailey Junior, there's no reason for you to be crying just because you got something from Vivian and Big Bailey." When we still didn't force ourselves to answer, she asked, "You want me to tell Santa Claus to take these things back?" I wanted to scream, "Yes. Tell him to take them back." But I didn't move.

Later Bailey and I talked. He said that if the things really did come from Mother, maybe it meant that she was getting ready to come and get us. Maybe she had just been angry at something we had done, but was forgiving us and would send for us soon. Bailey and I tore the insides out of the doll the day after Christmas, but he warned me that I had to keep the tea set in good condition because any day or night she might come riding up.

♦

A year later our father came to Stamps without warning. It was awful for Bailey and me to meet the reality so suddenly. We, or at least I, had built such strong dreams about him and our mysterious mother that seeing him tore my inventions apart like a hard pull on a paper chain. He arrived in front of the Store in a clean gray car. (He must have stopped just outside of town to wipe it in preparation for the "grand entrance.") His bigness shocked me. His shoulders were so wide I thought he'd have trouble getting in the door. He was taller than anyone I had seen, and he was almost fat. His clothes were too small too. And he was extremely handsome. Momma cried, "Bailey, my baby. Great God, Bailey." And Uncle Willie stuttered, "Bu-Buh-Bailey." My brother said, "I don't believe it. It's him. It's our daddy." And my seven-year-old world fell apart, and would never be put back together again.

He spoke perfect English, like the school principal, and even better. He had the attitude of a man who did not believe what he heard or what he himself was saying. "So this is Daddy's little man? Boy, anybody tell you that you look like me?" He had Bailey in one arm and me in the other. "And Daddy's little girl. You've been good children, haven't you?"

I was so proud of him that it was hard to wait for the gossip to get around that he was in town. Wouldn't the kids be surprised at how handsome our daddy was? And that he loved us enough to come down to Stamps to visit? Everyone could tell from the way he talked and from the car and clothes that he was rich and maybe had a castle in California. (I later learned that he had been a doorman at Santa Monica's fancy Breakers Hotel.) Then the possibility of being compared with him occurred to me, and I didn't want anyone to see him. Maybe he wasn't my real father. Bailey was his son, no doubt, but I was an orphan that they adopted to provide Bailey with company.

For three weeks the Store was filled with people who had gone to school with him or heard about him. Then one day he said he had to get back to California. It was a relief. My world was going to be emptier and less interesting, but the silent threat of his leaving someday would be gone. I wouldn't have to wonder whether I loved him or not, or to answer, "Does Daddy's baby want to go to California with Daddy?" Bailey had told him that he wanted to go, but I had kept quiet. Momma was glad too, although she had had a good time cooking special things for him and showing her California son to the poor people of Arkansas. But Uncle Willie was suffering from our father's presence, and like a mother bird Momma was more concerned with her crippled child than the one who could fly away from the nest.

He was going to take us with him! The knowledge swam through my days and made me both excited and nervous. My thoughts quickly changed. Now this way, now that, now the other. Should I go with my father? Should I beg Momma to let me stay with her? Did I have the courage to try life without Bailey? I couldn't decide.

Momma cut down a few give-aways that had been traded to her by white women's servants, and spent long nights in the dining room sewing dresses and skirts for me. She looked pretty sad, but each time I found her watching me she'd say, as if I had already disobeyed, "You be a good girl now. You hear?" She would have been more surprised than I if she'd taken me in her arms and cried at losing me. Her world was bordered on all sides by work, duty, religion, and "her place." I don't think she ever knew that a deep love hung over everything she touched. In later years I asked her if she loved me and she avoided answering by saying, "God is love. Just worry about whether you're being a good girl, then He will love you."

♦

I sat in the back of the car, with Dad's leather suitcases and our boxes. There wasn't enough room to stretch. Whenever he thought about it, Dad asked, "Are you comfortable back there, Daddy's baby?" He never waited to hear my answer, which was "Yes, sir," before he'd continue his conversation with Bailey. He and Bailey told jokes, and Bailey laughed all the time and put out Dad's cigarettes.

I was angry with Bailey. There was no doubt he was trying to be friends with Dad; he even started to laugh like him.

"How are you going to feel seeing your mother? Going to be happy?" he was asking Bailey, but I understood and was concerned. Were we going to see Her? I thought we were going to California. I was suddenly afraid. Would she laugh at us the way he did? How would we feel if she had other children now, whom she kept with her? I said, "I want to go back to Stamps." Dad laughed, "You mean you don't want to go to St. Louis to see your mother? She's not going to eat you, you know."

He turned to Bailey and I looked at the side of his face; he was so unreal to me that I felt as if I were watching a doll talk. "Bailey Junior, ask your sister why she wants to go back to Stamps." He sounded more like a white man than a Negro. Maybe he was the only brown-skinned white man in the world. But Bailey was quiet for the first time since we left Stamps. I guess he was thinking about seeing Mother. How could an eight-year-old contain that much fear? He holds it in his throat, he tightens his feet and closes the fear between his toes.

"Junior, ask her. What do you think your mother will say, when I tell her that her children didn't want to see her?" The thought that he *would* tell her shook me and Bailey at the same time. He leaned over the back of the seat toward me—"You know you want to see Mother Dear. Don't cry." Dad laughed and asked himself, I guess, "What will she say to that?"

I stopped crying since there was no chance to get back to Stamps and Momma. Bailey wasn't going to support me, I could tell, so I decided to shut up, stop crying, and wait for whatever seeing Mother Dear was going to bring.

♦

To describe my mother would be to write about a storm in its perfect power. We had been received by her mother and had waited on the edge of our seats in the overfurnished living room. (Dad talked easily with our grandmother, as whitefolks talk to Blacks, unembarrassed and never apologizing.) We were both fearful of Mother's coming and impatient at her delay.

23

It is remarkable how much truth there is in the expression "love at first sight." My mother's beauty astonished me. Her red lips (Momma said it was a sin to wear lipstick) split to show even white teeth. Her smile widened her mouth beyond her cheeks, beyond her ears, and seemingly through the walls to the street outside. I was speechless. I knew immediately why she had sent me away. She was too beautiful to have children. I had never seen a woman as pretty as she who was called "Mother."

Bailey fell immediately and for ever in love. I saw his eyes shining like hers; he had forgotten the loneliness and the nights when we had cried together because we were "unwanted children." He had never left her warm side. She was his Mother Dear and I accepted his condition. They were more alike than she and I, or even he and I. They both had physical beauty and personality.

Our father left St. Louis a few days later for California, and I was neither glad nor sorry. He was a stranger, and if he chose to leave us with a stranger, it made no difference.

♦

Grandmother Baxter was nearly white. She had come to St. Louis at the turn of the century to study nursing. While she was working at Homer G. Phillips Hospital she met and married Grandfather Baxter. She was white (having no features that could be called Negro) and he was Black. Their marriage was a happy one.

The Negro section of St. Louis in the mid-thirties had everything. Drinking and gambling were so obviously practiced that it was hard for me to believe that they were against the law. Bailey and I, as newcomers, were quickly told by our schoolmates who the men on the street corners and outside the bars were as we passed.

We met the gamblers and whiskey salesmen not only in the

loud streets but in our orderly living room as well. They were often there when we returned from school, sitting with hats in their hands, as we had done on our arrival in the big city. They waited silently for Grandmother Baxter.

Her white skin brought her a great deal of respect. Moreover, the reputation of her six mean children and the fact that she was in charge of voting in her district gave her the power to deal with even the lowest crook without fear. If she helped them, they knew what would be expected of them. At election time, they were expected to bring in the votes from their neighborhood. And they always did.

St. Louis also introduced me to thin-sliced meat, lettuce on sandwich bread, and family loyalty. In Arkansas, where we preserved our own meat, we ate half-inch slices for breakfast, but in St. Louis we bought paper-thin slices and ate them in sandwiches. In Stamps, lettuce was used only to make a bed for potato salad.

When we entered Toussaint L'Ouverture Elementary School, we were struck by the ignorance of the other students and the rudeness of our teachers. Only the vastness of the building impressed us; not even the white school in Stamps was as large.

The students, however, were shockingly behind us in their skills. Bailey and I did math at an advanced level because of our work in the Store, and we read well because in Stamps there wasn't anything else to do. We were moved up a grade because our teachers thought that we country children would make the other students feel inferior—and we did. We learned to say "Yes" and "No" rather than "Yes, ma'am," and "No, ma'am."

Occasionally Mother, whom we seldom saw in the house, told us to meet her at Louie's, the bar she worked in. We used to come in the back door, and the smell of beer, steam, and boiling meat made me feel sick. Mother had cut my hair short like hers and straightened it, so my head felt skinned and the back of my

25

neck so bare that I was ashamed to have anyone walk up behind me.

At Louie's we were greeted by Mother's friends as "Bibbie's darling babies" and were given soft drinks and boiled meat. While we sat on the wooden benches, Mother would dance alone in front of us to music from the radio. I loved her most at those times. She was like a pretty kiss that floated just above my head.

♦

The family was proud of the Baxter loyalty. Uncle Tommy said that even the children felt it before they were old enough to be taught. They told us the story of Bailey teaching me to walk when he was less than three. Displeased with my awkward motions, he was supposed to have said, "This is *my* sister. *I* have to teach her to walk." They also told me how I got the name "My." After Bailey learned definitely that I was his sister, he refused to call me Marguerite, but addressed me each time as "Mya Sister," which was shortened to "My." In later years it was lengthened to "Maya."

We lived in a big house on Caroline Street with our grandparents for half the year before Mother moved us in with her. Moving from the house where the family was centered meant nothing to me. It was just a small pattern in the grand design of our lives. The new house was not stranger than the other, except that we were with Mother.

Bailey called her "Mother Dear" until our nearness softened the phrase's formality to "M'Deah." I could never completely understand her realness. She was so pretty and so quick that even when she had just awakened, I thought she was beautiful.

Mother had prepared a place for us, and we went into it gratefully. We each had a room, plenty to eat, and store-bought clothes to wear. And after all, she didn't have to do it. If we annoyed her or were disobedient, she could always send us back to Stamps. The weight of appreciation and the threat, which was never spoken, of a return to Momma were burdens I couldn't think about.

Mother's boyfriend, Mr. Freeman, lived with us, or we lived with him. (I never quite knew which.) He was a Southerner, too, and big. But a little fat. Even if Mother hadn't been such a pretty woman, light-skinned with straight hair, he was lucky to get her, and he knew it. She was educated, from a well-known family, and after all, wasn't she born in St. Louis? She laughed all the time and made jokes. He was grateful. I think he must have been many years older than she, but if not, he still had the inferiority of old men married to younger women. He watched every move she made, and when she left the room, his eyes didn't want to let her go.

Chapter 6　Mr. Freeman

I had decided that St. Louis was a foreign country. I would never get used to the sounds of water going down the toilets, or the packaged foods, or doorbells, or the noise of cars and trains and buses. In my mind I only stayed in St. Louis for a few weeks. As quickly as I understood that I had not reached my home, I returned to the storybook world of Robin Hood, where all reality was unreal and even that changed every day. I had the same attitude that I had used in Stamps: "I didn't come to stay."

Mother was good at providing for us. Although she was a nurse, she never worked at her profession while we were with her. Mr. Freeman brought in the necessities and she earned extra money working in gambling houses. The regular eight-to-five world didn't have enough excitement for her, and it was twenty years later that I first saw her in a nurse's uniform.

Mr. Freeman was a manager in the Southern Pacific train yards and came home late sometimes, after Mother had gone out. He took his dinner off the stove, where she had carefully covered it and which she had warned us not to touch. He ate quietly in the kitchen while Bailey and I read separately and greedily our own Street & Smith* magazine. We had spending money now and bought magazines with colorful pictures. When Mother was away, we were put on the honor system. We had to finish our homework, eat dinner, and wash the dishes before we could read or listen to the radio.

Mr. Freeman moved gracefully, like a big brown bear, and seldom spoke to us. He just waited for Mother and put his whole self into the waiting. He never read the paper or tapped his foot to the radio. He waited. That was all.

If she came home before we went to bed, we saw the man come alive. He would jump out of the big chair, like a man coming out of sleep, smiling. When her key opened the door, Mr. Freeman would have already asked his usual question, "Hey, Bibbi, have a good time?"

His question would hang in the air while she ran over to kiss him on the lips. Then she turned to Bailey and me with the lipstick kisses. "Haven't you finished your homework?" If we had and were just reading—"OK, say your prayers and go to bed." If we hadn't—"Then go to your room and finish . . . then say your prayers and go to bed."

Mr. Freeman's smile never grew, it stayed the same. Sometimes Mother would go over and sit on his lap, and the grin on his face looked as if it would stay there for ever.

Because of the stories we read and our lively imaginations and, probably, memories of our brief but full lives, Bailey and I suffered—he physically and I mentally. He stuttered, and I sweated

* Street & Smith: a company that produced very popular books and magazines, especially fiction.

through frightening dreams. He was constantly told to slow down and start again, and on my particularly bad nights my mother would take me in to sleep with her, in the large bed with Mr. Freeman. After the third time in Mother's bed, I thought there was nothing strange about sleeping there.

One morning she got out of bed early, and I fell back asleep again. But I awoke to a pressure, a strange feeling on my left leg. It was too soft to be a hand, and it wasn't the touch of clothes. Whatever it was, I hadn't experienced it in all the years of sleeping with Momma. It didn't move, and I was too surprised to. I turned my head a little to the left to see if Mr. Freeman was awake and gone, but his eyes were open and both hands were above the cover. I knew, as if I had always known, that it was his "thing" on my leg.

He said, "Just stay right here, Ritie, I ain't gonna* hurt you." I wasn't afraid—a little uncertain, maybe, but not afraid. Of course I knew that lots of people did "it" and that they used their "things" to do this deed, but no one I knew had ever done it to anybody. Mr. Freeman pulled me to him, and put his hand between my legs. He didn't hurt, but Momma had always said: "Keep your legs closed, and don't let nobody see between them."

"Now, I didn't hurt you. Don't get scared." He threw back the blankets and his "thing" stood up like a brown ear of corn. He took my hand and said, "Feel it." Then he dragged me on top of his chest with his left arm, and his right hand was moving so fast and his heart was beating so hard that I was afraid he would die.

Finally he was quiet, and then came the nice part. He held me so softly that I wished he wouldn't let me go. I felt at home. From the way he was holding me I knew he'd never let me go or let anything bad ever happen to me. This was probably my real father and we had found each other at last. But then he rolled over, leaving me in a wet place, and stood up.

* gonna: short for "going to"

29

"I have to talk to you, Ritie." He pulled off his shorts, which had fallen to his ankles, and went into the bathroom.

It was true the bed was wet, but I knew I hadn't had an accident. Maybe Mr. Freeman had one while he was holding me. He came back with a glass of water and told me in a sour voice, "Get up. You peed in the bed." He poured water on the wet spot, and it did look like my bed on many mornings.

Having lived in Southern strictness, I knew when to keep quiet around adults, but I did want to ask him why he said I peed when I was sure he didn't believe that. If he thought I was naughty, would that mean that he would never hold me again? Or admit that he was my father? I had made him ashamed of me.

"Ritie, you love Bailey?" He sat down on the bed and I came close, hoping. "Yes." He was bending down, pulling on his socks, and his back was so large and friendly I wanted to rest my head on it.

"If you ever tell anybody what we did, I'll have to kill Bailey."

What had we done? We? Obviously he didn't mean my peeing in the bed. I didn't understand and didn't dare ask him. There was no chance to ask Bailey either, because that would be telling what we had done. The thought that he might kill Bailey shocked me. After he left the room I thought about telling Mother that I hadn't peed in the bed. But then if she asked me what happened I'd have to tell her about Mr. Freeman holding me, and I couldn't do that.

For weeks after that he said nothing to me, except brief hellos which were given without ever looking in my direction.

This was the first secret I had ever kept from Bailey and sometimes I thought he should be able to read it on my face, but he noticed nothing.

I began to feel lonely for Mr. Freeman and being wrapped in his big arms. Before, my world had been Bailey, food, Momma, the Store, reading books, and Uncle Willie. Now, for the first time, it included physical contact.

I began to wait for Mr. Freeman to come in from the yards, but when he did he never noticed me, although I put a lot of feeling into "Good evening, Mr. Freeman."

One evening, when I couldn't concentrate on anything, I went over to him and sat quickly on his lap. He had been waiting for Mother again. Bailey was listening to the radio and didn't miss me. At first Mr. Freeman sat still, not holding me or anything, then I felt a soft lump under my thigh begin to move. It hit against me and started to harden. Then he pulled me to his chest. He smelled of coal dust and grease, and he was so close I buried my face in his shirt and listened to his heart. It was beating just for me. Only I could hear it, only I could feel the jumping on my face. He said, "Sit still, stop moving around." But all the time, he pushed me around on his lap, then suddenly he stood up and I slipped to the floor. He ran to the bathroom.

For months he stopped speaking to me again. I was hurt and for a time felt lonelier than ever, but then I forgot about him.

♦

I read more than ever, and wished in my soul that I had been born a boy. Horatio Alger was the greatest writer in the world. His heroes were always good, always won, and were always boys. I could have developed the first two qualities, but becoming a boy was sure to be difficult, if not impossible.

When spring came to St. Louis, I took out my first library card, and since Bailey and I seemed to be growing apart, I spent most of my Saturdays at the library. The little princesses who were mistaken for servants became more real to me than our house, our mother, our school, or Mr. Freeman.

During those months we saw our grandparents and our uncles, but they usually asked the same question, "Have you been good children?" for which there was only one answer. Even Bailey wouldn't have dared to answer "No."

♦

On a late spring Saturday, after our chores (nothing like those in Stamps) were done, Bailey and I were going out, he to play baseball and I to the library. Mr. Freeman said to me, after Bailey had gone downstairs, "Ritie, go get some milk for the house."

He gave me money and I rushed to the store and back to the house. After putting the milk in the refrigerator, I turned and had just reached the front door when I heard, "Ritie." He was sitting in the big chair by the radio. "Ritie, come here." I didn't think about the holding time until I got close to him. His pants were open and his "thing" was standing out of them by itself.

"No, sir, Mr. Freeman." I started to back away. I didn't want to touch that thing again, and I didn't need him to hold me anymore. He grabbed my arm and pulled me between his legs. His face was still and looked kind, but he didn't smile. He did nothing, except reach his left hand around to turn on the radio without even looking at it. Over the noise of the music, he said, "Now, this ain't gonna hurt you much. You liked it before, didn't you?"

I didn't want to admit that I had in fact liked him holding me or that I had liked his smell or the hard heart-beating, so I said nothing. And his face became mean.

His legs were squeezing my waist. "Pull down your underpants." I hesitated for two reasons: he was holding me too tight to move, and I was sure that any minute my mother or Bailey would run in the door and save me.

"We were just playing before." He released me enough to pull down my underpants, and then dragged me closer to him. Turning the radio up loud, too loud, he said, "If you scream, I'm gonna kill you. And if you tell, I'm gonna kill Bailey." I could tell he meant what he said. I couldn't understand why he wanted to kill my brother. Neither of us had done anything to him. And then.

32

Then there was the pain. A breaking and entering when even the senses are torn apart. The act of rape on an eight-year-old body is a matter of the child's body breaking open, because the body can, and the mind of the rapist cannot stop.

I thought I had died—I woke up in a white-walled world, and it had to be heaven. But Mr. Freeman was there and he was washing me. His hands shook, but he held me upright in the tub and washed my legs. "I didn't mean to hurt you, Ritie. I didn't mean it. But don't you tell . . . Remember, don't you tell anyone."

I felt cool and very clean and just a little tired. "No, sir, Mr. Freeman, I won't tell." I was somewhere above everything. "But I'm so tired I'll just go and lay down a while, please," I whispered to him. I thought if I spoke out loud, he might become frightened and hurt me again. He dried me and handed me my underpants. "Put these on and go to the library. Your mother ought to be coming home soon. You just act normal."

Walking down the street, I felt the wet on my underpants and my body hurt between my legs. I couldn't sit long on the hard seats in the library, so I walked by the empty lot where Bailey played ball, but he wasn't there. I stood for a while and watched the older boys playing and then headed home.

After two blocks, I knew I'd never make it. Not unless I counted every step. I had started to burn between my legs. The insides of my thighs shook. I went up the stairs one step at a time. No one was in the living room, so I went straight to bed, after hiding my red-and-yellow stained underpants under the sheets.

When Mother came in she said, "Well, young lady, I believe this is the first time I've seen you go to bed without being told. You must be sick."

I wasn't sick, but the pit of my stomach was on fire—how could I tell her that? Bailey came in later and asked me what the matter was. There was nothing to tell him. When Mother called us to eat and I said I wasn't hungry, she laid her cool hand on my

33

forehead and cheeks. After she took my temperature, she said, "You have a little fever."

Mr. Freeman took up the whole doorway. "Then Bailey ought not to be in there with her. Unless you want a whole house full of sick children." She walked by Mr. Freeman. "Come on, Junior. Get some cool towels and wipe your sister's face."

As Bailey left the room, Mr. Freeman advanced to the bed. He leaned over, his whole face a threat. "If you tell . . ." And again so softly, I almost didn't hear it—"If you tell." I didn't have the energy to answer him. He had to know that I wasn't going to tell anything. Bailey came in with the towels and Mr. Freeman walked out.

That night I kept waking to hear Mother and Mr. Freeman arguing. I couldn't hear what they were saying, but I did hope that she wouldn't make him so mad that he'd hurt her too. I knew he could do it, with his cold face and empty eyes.

Maybe I slept, but soon morning was there and Mother was pretty over my bed. "How're you feeling, baby?"

"Fine, Mother." An automatic answer. "Where's Bailey?"

She said he was still asleep but that she hadn't slept all night. She had been in and out of my room, checking on me. I asked her where Mr. Freeman was, and her face filled with remembered anger. "He's gone. Moved this morning."

Could I tell her now? The terrible pain assured me that I couldn't. What he did to me, and what I allowed, must have been very bad if already God let me hurt so much. If Mr. Freeman was gone, did that mean Bailey was out of danger? And if so, if I told him, would he still love me?

That Sunday goes and comes in my memory. Once Bailey was reading to me, and then Mother was looking closely at my face. Then there was a doctor who took my temperature and held my wrist.

"Bailey!" I supposed I had screamed—he appeared suddenly,

and I asked him to help me and we'd run away to California or France or Chicago. I knew that I was dying. In fact, I longed for death, but I didn't want to die anywhere near Mr. Freeman. I knew that even now he wouldn't have allowed death to take me unless he wished it to.

Mother said I should be bathed and the sheets had to be changed since I had sweat so much. But when they tried to move me I fought, and even Bailey couldn't hold me. Then she picked me up in her arms and the terror lessened for a while. Bailey began to change the bed. As he pulled off the wet sheets he found the underpants I had hidden. They fell at Mother's feet.

In the hospital, Bailey told me that I had to tell who did that to me, or the man would hurt another little girl. When I explained that I couldn't tell because the man would kill him, Bailey said knowingly, "He can't kill me. I won't let him." And of course I believed him. Bailey didn't lie to me. So I told him.

Bailey cried at the side of my bed until I started to cry too. Almost fifteen years passed before I saw my brother cry like that again.

Using the brain he was born with (those were his words later that day), he gave his information to Grandmother Baxter. Mr. Freeman was arrested, avoiding the awful anger of my uncles.

I would have liked to stay in the hospital the rest of my life. Mother brought flowers and candy. Grandmother came with fruit and my uncles walked around my bed, guarding me. When they were able to bring Bailey in, he read to me for hours.

♦

The court was filled. Some people even stood behind the benches at the back. Grandmother Bailey's clients were there. The gamblers and their women whispered to me that I now knew as much as they did. I was eight, and grown. I sat with my family (Bailey couldn't come) and they rested still on their seats. Unmoving.

Poor Mr. Freeman turned in his chair to look empty threats over to me. He didn't know that he couldn't kill Bailey ... and Bailey didn't lie ... to me.

"Was that the first time the accused touched you?" Mr. Freeman's lawyer asked. The question stopped me. Mr. Freeman had surely done something very wrong, but I was certain that I had helped him to do it. I didn't want to lie, but the lawyer wouldn't let me think, so I remained silent.

"Did the accused try to touch you before the time you say he raped you?"

I couldn't say yes and tell them how he had loved me once for a few minutes and how he had held me close before he thought I had peed in the bed. My uncles would kill me and Grandmother Baxter would stop speaking, as she often did when she was angry. And Mother, who thought I was such a good girl, would be so disappointed. But most important, there was Bailey. I had kept a big secret from him.

"Marguerite, answer the question. Did the accused touch you before the occasion on which you claim he raped you?"

Everyone in the court knew that the answer had to be "No." Everyone except Mr. Freeman and me. I looked at his face, and I said "No."

The lie lumped in my throat and I couldn't get air. How I hated the man for making me lie. The tears didn't comfort my heart as they usually did. I screamed, "Old, mean, dirty thing, you. Dirty old thing." Our lawyer brought me off the stand and into my mother's arms.

Mr. Freeman was given one year and one day, but he never got a chance to go to prison. His lawyer (or someone) got him released that very afternoon.

In the living room, Bailey and I played a board game on the floor. I played badly because I was thinking how I would be able to tell Bailey that I had lied and, even worse for our relationship, kept a secret from him. Bailey answered the doorbell, because Grandmother was in the kitchen. A tall white policeman asked for Mrs. Baxter. Had they found out about the lie? Maybe the policeman was coming to put me in jail because I had sworn on the Bible that everything I said would be the truth, the whole truth. The man in our living room was taller than the sky and whiter than my image of God.

"Mrs. Baxter, I thought you ought to know. Freeman's been found dead on the lot behind the meat factory."

Softly, she said, "Poor man." She wiped her hands on the dishtowel and just as softly asked, "Do they know who did it?"

The policeman said, "Seems like he was dropped there. Some say he was kicked to death."

Grandmother's face turned a little red. "Tom, thanks for telling me. Poor man. Well, maybe it's better this way."

And he was gone, and a man was dead because I lied. Where was the balance in that? One lie surely wouldn't be worth a man's life. Bailey could have explained it all to me, but I didn't care to ask him. Obviously I had given up my place in heaven for ever and I had no courage. I could feel the evil flowing through my body and waiting to rush off my tongue if I tried to open my mouth. I held my teeth tightly shut. If it escaped, wouldn't it flood the world and all the innocent people?

Grandmother Baxter said, "Ritie and Junior, you didn't hear a thing. I never want this situation nor that man's evil name mentioned in this house again. I mean that." She went back into the kitchen to make apple pie for my celebration.

Even Bailey looked frightened. He sat alone, looking at a man's death. Not quite understanding it but frightened anyway.

In those moments I decided that although Bailey loved me, he couldn't help. I had sold myself to the Devil and there could be no escape. The only thing I could do was to stop talking to everyone except Bailey. Somehow I knew that because I loved him so much I'd never hurt him, but if I talked to anyone else that person might die too.

I had to stop talking.

In the first weeks my family accepted my behavior as a post-rape, post-hospital problem. (Neither the word "rape" nor the experience was mentioned in Grandmother's house, where Bailey and I were again staying.) They understood that I could talk to Bailey, but to no one else.

Then came the last visit from the visiting nurse, and the doctor said I was healed. That meant that I should be back on the sidewalks playing ball or enjoying the games I had been given when I was sick. When I refused to be the child they knew, I was called impudent.

For a while I was punished for not speaking; and then came the whippings, given by any relative who felt himself offended.

Chapter 7   Return to Stamps

We were on the train going back to Stamps, and this time I had to comfort Bailey. He cried for hours as he walked down the coach, and pressed his little-boy body against the window looking for a last quick view of his Mother Dear.

I have never known if Momma sent for us, or if the St. Louis family had just had enough of my unpleasant presence. I cared less about the trip than about the fact that Bailey was unhappy, and had no more thought of our destination than if I had been only heading for the toilet.

The quietness of Stamps was exactly what I wanted, without knowing it. After St. Louis, with its noise and activity, its trucks and buses, and loud family gatherings, I welcomed the quiet streets and lonely little houses in dirt yards.

The calmness of its residents encouraged me to relax. They

showed me contentment based on the belief that nothing more was coming to them, although a great deal more was due. Their decision to be satisfied with life's unfairness was a lesson for me. Entering Stamps, I had the feeling that I was stepping over the border lines of the map and would fall, without fear, right off the end of the world. Nothing more could happen because in Stamps nothing happened.

I crept into this shelter.

For a long time, nothing was demanded of me or of Bailey. We were, after all, Mrs. Henderson's California grandchildren, and had been away on an exciting trip way up North to the fabulous St. Louis. Our father had come the year before, driving a big, shiny car and speaking with a big city accent, so all we had to do was stay quiet for months and enjoy the benefits of our adventures.

People, including all the children, made regular trips to the Store, "just to see the travelers."

They stood around and asked, "Well, how is it up North?"

"See any of those big buildings?"

"Were you scared?"

"Whitefolks any different, like they say?"

Bailey answered every question, and from a corner of his lively imagination told a story that I was sure was as unreal to him as it was to me.

Momma, knowing Bailey, warned, "Now, Junior, be careful you don't tell a not true." (Nice people didn't say "lie.")

"Everybody wears new clothes and has an inside toilet. Some people have refrigerators. The snow is so deep you can get buried right outside your door and people won't find you for a year. We made ice cream out of the snow." That was the only fact that I could have supported. During the winter, we had collected a bowl of snow and poured canned milk over it, put sugar on top, and called it ice cream.

Momma grinned and Uncle Willie was proud when Bailey entertained the customers with our experiences. We brought people into the Store, and everyone loved us. Our journey to magical places was a colorful addition to the town, and our return made us even more the most enviable of people.

I never knew if Uncle Willie had been told about the incident in St. Louis, but sometimes I caught him watching me with a far-off look in his big eyes. Then he would quickly send me on some errand that would take me out of his presence. When that happened I was happy and ashamed. I certainly didn't want a cripple's sympathy, nor did I want Uncle Willie, whom I loved, to think of me as being sinful or dirty. If he thought so, at least I didn't want to know it.

People, except Momma and Uncle Willie, accepted my unwillingness to talk as a natural result of an unwilling return to the South. And an indication that I missed the good times we had had in the big city. Also, I was well known for being "tender-hearted." Southern Negroes used that term to mean sensitive, and considered a person with that problem to be a little sick or in delicate health. So I was understood, if not forgiven.

Chapter 8   Two Women

For nearly a year I went around the house, the Store, the school, and the church without talking and keeping to myself. Then I met, or got to know, the lady who threw me my first lifeline.

Mrs. Bertha Flowers was the upper-class woman of Black Stamps. She had the grace to appear warm in the coldest weather, and on the hot Arkansas summer days she seemed cool. She was thin, and her printed dresses and flowered hats were as right for her as jeans for a farmer. Her skin was dark black. She wore gloves, too. She was our side of town's example of the richest woman in town.

I don't think I ever saw Mrs. Flowers laugh, but she smiled often. When she chose to smile on me, I always wanted to thank her. The action was so graceful and kind.

She was one of the few real ladies I have ever known, and has remained throughout my life the measure of what a human being can be.

Momma had a strange relationship with her. Most often when Mrs. Flowers passed on the road in front of the Store, she spoke to Momma in her soft voice: "Good day, Mrs. Henderson." Momma responded with: "How you, Sister Flowers?"

Mrs. Flowers didn't belong to our church, nor was she Momma's good friend. Why did she insist on calling her Sister Flowers? Shame made me want to hide my face. Mrs. Flowers deserved better than to be called Sister. Then, Momma left out the verb. Why not ask, "How *are* you, *Mrs*. Flowers?" I hated her for showing her ignorance to Mrs. Flowers. It didn't occur to me for many years that they were as alike as sisters, separated only by formal education.

Although I was upset, neither of the women was at all bothered by what I thought was an impolite greeting. Mrs. Flowers would continue her walk up the hill to her little house, and Momma kept on doing whatever had brought her to the front porch.

Occasionally, though, Mrs. Flowers would wander off the road and down to the Store and Momma would say to me, "Sister, you go on and play." As I left I would hear the beginning of a private conversation, Momma continuing to use the wrong verb, or none at all. But they talked, and from the side of the building where I waited, I heard their voices mixing together. They were interrupted from time to time by giggles that must have come from Mrs. Flowers (Momma never giggled in her life). Then she was gone.

She attracted me because she was like people I had never met personally. Like women in English novels who walked with their dogs. Like the women who sat in front of fireplaces, drinking tea and eating cookies. It would be safe to say that she made me proud to be Negro, just by being herself.

She acted just as well-mannered and civilized as whitefolks in the movies and books, and she was more beautiful. None of them could have come near that warm color without looking gray by comparison.

One summer afternoon, still fresh in my memory, she stopped at the Store to buy groceries. Another Negro woman of her health and age would have been expected to carry the paper sacks home in one hand, but Momma said, "Sister Flowers, I'll send Bailey up to your house with these things."

She smiled. "Thank you, Mrs. Henderson. I'd prefer Marguerite, though." My name was beautiful when she said it. "I've been meaning to talk to her, anyway."

Momma said, "Well, that's all right then. Sister, go and change your dress. You're going with Sister Flowers."

What did one put on to go to Mrs. Flowers' house? I knew I shouldn't put on a Sunday dress. It wouldn't be right. Certainly not a house dress, since I was already wearing a clean one. I chose a school dress, naturally. It was formal without suggesting that going to Mrs. Flowers' house was the same as attending church.

I walked back into the Store.

"Now, don't you look nice." I had chosen the right dress.

"Mrs. Henderson, you make most of the children's clothes, don't you?"

"Yes, ma'am. Sure do. Store-bought clothes ain't hardly worth the thread it takes to stitch them."

"You do a beautiful job, though, so neat. That dress looks professional."

Momma was enjoying the seldom-received praise. Since everyone we knew (except Mrs. Flowers, of course) could sew well, praise was rarely handed out for the commonly practiced skill.

"I try, with the help of the Lord, Sister Flowers, to finish the inside just like I do the outside. Come here, Sister."

She made me take off the dress. As they talked, I wouldn't look at either of them. Momma hadn't thought that taking off my dress in front of Mrs. Flowers would make me feel like dying. Mrs. Flowers, though, had known that I would be embarrassed and that was even worse. When Momma told me to, I put the dress back on, picked up the groceries, and went out to wait in the hot sunshine. It would be appropriate if I died before they came outside. Just dropped dead on the porch.

There was a little path beside the rocky road, and Mrs. Flowers walked in front, swinging her arms. She said, without turning her head, to me, "I hear you're doing very good school work, Marguerite, but that it's all written. The teachers report that they have trouble getting you to talk in class." The path widened to allow us to walk together, but I stayed behind.

"Come and walk along with me, Marguerite." I couldn't have refused even if I wanted to. She pronounced my name so nicely.

"Now, no one is going to make you talk—possibly no one can. But remember, language is man's way of communication with other people and it is language alone which separates him from the lower animals." That was a totally new idea to me, and I would need time to think about it.

"Your grandmother says you read a lot. That's good, but not good enough. Words mean more than what is written on paper. They need the human voice to give them deeper meaning."

I memorized the part about the human voice giving meaning to words. It seemed so true and poetic.

She said she was going to give me some books and that I not only must read them, I must read them aloud. She suggested that I try to make a sentence sound in as many different ways as possible.

"I'll accept no excuse if you return a book to me that has been badly handled." I couldn't imagine the punishment I would deserve if in fact I did abuse a book of Mrs. Flowers'. Death would be too kind and brief.

The smells in the house surprised me. Somehow I had never connected Mrs. Flowers with food or eating or any other common experience of ordinary people.

"I made cookies this morning. I had planned to invite you for cookies and lemonade so we could have this little chat."

She took the bags from me and disappeared through the kitchen door. I looked around the room that I had never in my wildest dreams imagined I would see.

"Have a seat, Marguerite. Over there by the table." She carried a plate covered with a small towel. I was certain that everything about her cookies would be perfect.

Remembering my manners, I took nice little lady-like bites off the edges. She said she had made them especially for me and that she had a few in the kitchen that I could take home to my brother. It was a dream come true.

As I ate she began the first of what we later called "my lessons in living." She said that I must always be intolerant of ignorance but understanding of a lack of knowledge. That some people, unable to go to school, were more educated and even more intelligent than college professors. She encouraged me to listen carefully to country people's sayings. In those sayings was wisdom collected through the years.

When I finished the cookies, she brushed off the table and brought a thick, small book from the bookcase. I had read *A Tale of Two Cities*, and it met my standards as a romantic novel.

She began to read. The way her voice said the words was nearly singing. When she finished reading, I hadn't really heard, heard to understand, a single word.

"How do you like that?"

It occurred to me that she expected a response. I had to speak.

I said, "Yes, ma'am." It was the least I could do, but it was the most also.

"There's one more thing. Take this book of poems and memorize one for me. Next time you visit, I want you to say it for me."

On that first day, I ran down the hill and into the road and had the good sense to stop running before I reached the Store.

I was liked, and what a difference it made. I was respected not as Mrs. Henderson's grandchild or Bailey's sister but for just being Marguerite Johnson. I didn't question why Mrs. Flowers had chosen me to give her attention to, nor did I realize that Momma might have asked her to talk to me. All I cared about was that she had made cookies for *me* and read to *me* from her favorite book. It was enough to prove that she liked me.

♦

Negro girls in small Southern towns were given as thorough and irrelevant preparations for adulthood as rich white girls shown in magazines. Admittedly the training was not the same. While white girls learned to dance and sit gracefully with a teacup balanced on their knees, we learned to sew designs on dishtowels, pillowcases, and handkerchiefs. It was understood that all girls could iron and wash, but the more skilled tasks around the home, like setting a table, baking meat, and cooking vegetables without meat, had to be learned elsewhere. Usually at the source of those habits. During my tenth year, a white woman's kitchen became my school.

Mrs. Viola Cullinan was a fat woman who lived in a three-bedroom house. She was unattractive until she smiled. Then the lines around her eyes and mouth disappeared, and her face looked friendly. She usually saved her smile until late afternoon when her woman friends dropped in and Miss Glory, the cook, served them cold drinks on the closed-in porch.

Miss Glory was very patient with me. She explained the different kinds of dishes. It took me a week to learn the difference between a salad plate, a bread plate, and a dessert plate. There were ice-cream glasses, wine glasses, green glass coffee cups with matching saucers, and water glasses. I was fascinated with them, with Mrs. Cullinan and her wonderful house.

On our way home one evening, Miss Glory told me that Mrs. Cullinan couldn't have children. She said that the doctor had taken out all her lady parts. If Mrs. Cullinan was walking around without those essentials, it explained why she drank alcohol out of unmarked bottles. I felt pity for her. Mrs. Cullinan didn't know what she missed. Or maybe she did. Poor Mrs. Cullinan.

For weeks I arrived early, left late, and tried very hard to make up for her childlessness. If she had had her own children, she wouldn't have had to ask me to run a thousand errands from her back door to the back doors of her friends. Poor old Mrs. Cullinan.

Then one evening Miss Glory told me to serve the ladies on the porch. After I set the plate down and turned toward the kitchen, one of the woman asked, "What's your name, girl?"

Mrs. Cullinan said, "She doesn't talk much. Her name's Margaret. As I understand it, she can talk when she wants to but she's usually quiet as a little mouse. Aren't you, Margaret?"

I smiled at her. Poor thing. No lady parts and she couldn't even pronounce my name correctly.

"She's a sweet little thing, though."

"Well, that may be, but the name's too long. I'd never bother myself. I'd call her Mary if I was you."

I was angry all the way to the kitchen. That terrible woman would never have the chance to call me Mary because if I was starving I'd never work for her. Giggles came in off the porch. I wondered what they could be laughing about.

Whitefolks were so strange. Could they be talking about me?

Everybody knew that they shared more information than Negroes did. It was possible that Mrs. Cullinan had friends in St. Louis who heard about a girl from Stamps being in court and wrote to tell her. Maybe she knew about Mr. Freeman.

I felt sick, and Miss Glory told me to go home. I realized how foolish I was being before I got there. Of course Mrs. Cullinan didn't know. Otherwise she wouldn't have given me the two nice dresses that Momma cut down, and she certainly wouldn't have called me a "sweet little thing." My stomach felt fine, and I didn't mention anything to Momma.

That evening I decided to write a poem about being white, fat, old, and without children. It was going to be a tragic poem. I would have to watch her carefully to capture her loneliness and pain.

The next day, she called me by the wrong name. Miss Glory and I were washing the lunch dishes when Mrs. Cullinan came to the doorway. "Mary?"

Miss Glory asked, "Who?"

Mrs. Cullinan knew and I knew. "I want Mary to go down to Mrs. Randall's and take her some soup. She's not been feeling well for a few days."

Miss Glory's face was a wonder to see. "You mean Margaret, ma'am. Her name's Margaret."

"That's too long. She's Mary now. Heat that soup from last night and put it in the large bowl. Mary, I want you to carry it carefully."

Every person I knew had a horror of being "called out of his name." Miss Glory felt sorry for me for a second. Then, as she handed me the soup bowl, she said, "Don't you mind, don't pay attention to that. Sticks and stones may break your bones, but words will never hurt you. You know, I've been working for her for twenty years."

She held the back door open for me. "Twenty years. I wasn't

47

much older than you. My name used to be Hallelujah. That's what my momma named me, but my boss gave me 'Glory,' and it stuck. I like it better, too."

I was in the little path that ran behind the houses when Miss Glory shouted, "It's shorter too."

For a few seconds I wasn't sure whether I would laugh (imagine being named Hallelujah) or cry (imagine letting some white woman rename you for her convenience). I had to leave the job, but the problem was going to be how to do it. Momma wouldn't allow me to leave for just any reason.

For a week, I looked into Mrs. Cullinan's face as she called me Mary. She ignored my coming late and leaving early. Miss Glory was a little annoyed because I had begun to leave egg on the dishes. I hoped that she would complain to our boss, but she didn't.

Then Bailey solved my problem. He had me describe the contents of her cupboard and the particular plates she liked best. I kept his instructions in mind. On the next day when Miss Glory was hanging out clothes and I had again been told to serve the old ladies on the porch, I dropped the empty serving plate. When I heard Mrs. Cullinan scream, "Mary!" I picked up her favorite dish and two of the green glass cups in readiness. As she entered the kitchen door, I let them fall on the floor.

She crawled around the floor and picked up pieces of the cups and cried, "Oh, Momma. Oh, dear God. It's Momma's dishes from Virginia. Oh, Momma, I'm sorry."

Miss Glory came running in from the yard and the women from the porch crowded around. Miss Glory was almost as upset as her boss. "You mean to say she broke our Virginia dishes? What are we gonna do?"

Mrs. Cullinan cried louder, "That clumsy nigger. Clumsy little black nigger."

The old woman who had first named me Mary leaned

down and asked, "Who did it, Viola? Was it Mary? Who did it?"

Everything was happening so fast I can't remember whether her action or her words came first, but I know that Mrs. Cullinan said, "Her name's Margaret, damn it, her name's Margaret." And she threw a piece of the broken plate at me.

I left the door wide open so all the neighbors could hear.

Mrs. Cullinan was right about one thing. My name wasn't Mary.

Chapter 9   Friends

Weekdays were the same. Saturdays, however, always dared to be different. After our return from St. Louis, Momma gave us a little cash weekly. I usually gave my money to Bailey, who went to the movies almost every Saturday. He brought back cowboy books for me.

One Saturday Bailey was late returning. Momma had begun heating water for the Saturday-night baths, and all the evening chores were done. It was quite late.

Uncle Willie said, "Sister, turn on the light." On Saturdays we used the electric lights so that last-minute shoppers could look down the hill and see if the Store was open. Momma hadn't told me to turn them on because she didn't want to believe that it was night and Bailey was still out in the dark. Her anxiety was obvious in her hurried movements around the kitchen and in her lonely fearful eyes. Any break from routine may result in terrible news.

I had very little pity for my relatives' anxiety. If something had happened to Bailey, Uncle Willie would always have Momma, and Momma had the Store. We weren't their children. But I would be the major loser if Bailey was dead—he was the only family I claimed, if not all I had.

"Momma," Uncle Willie called and she jumped. "Momma, why don't you and Sister walk down to meet him?"

Bailey's name hadn't been mentioned for hours, but we all knew whom he meant.

Of course. Why didn't that occur to me? I wanted to be gone. Momma said, "Wait a minute, little lady. Go get your sweater, and bring me mine."

It was darker in the road than I'd thought it would be. Momma told me to carry the flashlight and she reached for my hand. Her voice came from high above me and in the dark her hand was wrapped around mine. I loved her suddenly. She said nothing. Just the gentle pressure of her rough hand showed me her own concern and assurance.

We passed houses which I knew well by daylight but couldn't remember in the dark. Then Momma's hand tightened and let go, and I saw the small figure walking along, tired and old-mannish, his hands in his pockets and his head bent.

"Bailey," I said as Momma said, "Junior." I started to run, but her hand caught mine again and held it tight. "We'll walk, just like we've been walking, young lady." There was no chance to warn Bailey that he was dangerously late, that everybody had been worried, and that he should create a good lie, or, better, a great one.

Momma said, "Bailey, Junior," and he looked up without surprise. "You know it's night and you're just getting home?"

"Yes, ma'am." He was empty. Where was his excuse?

"What have you been doing?"

"Nothing."

"That's all you've got to say?"

"Yes, ma'am."

"All right, young man. We'll see when you get home."

She had let me go. I grabbed for Bailey's hand, but he pulled it away. I said, "Hey, Bailey," hoping to remind him that I was his sister and his only friend, but he said something like "Leave me alone."

Momma didn't turn on the flashlight on the way back, nor did she answer the "Good evenings" that greeted us as we passed the darkened houses.

I was confused and frightened. He was going to get a whipping and maybe he had done something terrible. If he couldn't talk to me it must have been serious. He seemed sad. I didn't know what to think.

Uncle Willie said, "Think you're getting too old, do you? You can't come home. You want to worry your grandmother to death?" Bailey was beyond fear. Uncle Willie had a leather belt in his good hand but Bailey didn't notice or didn't care. "I'm going to whip you this time." Our uncle had only whipped us once before and then only with a stick, so maybe now he was going to kill my brother. I screamed and grabbed for the belt, but Momma caught me. "He has a lesson coming to him. You come on and get your bath."

From the kitchen I heard the belt hit bare skin. Bailey made no sound. I was too afraid to splash water or even to cry and take a chance of not hearing Bailey's cries for help. But the cries never came and the whipping was finally over.

I lay awake for a long time, waiting for a sign—a cry or a whisper—from the next room telling me that he was still alive. Just before I fell exhausted into sleep, I heard Bailey saying his prayers: "Now I lay me down to sleep . . ."

My last memory of that night was the question, Why is he saying the baby prayer? We had been saying the grown-up prayer for years.

For days the Store was a strange place. Bailey didn't talk, smile, or apologize. His eyes were expressionless. At meals I tried to give him the best pieces of meat and the largest portion of dessert, but he wouldn't accept them.

Then one evening when we were feeding the pigs he said without warning, "I saw Mother Dear."

If he said it, it was the truth. He wouldn't lie to me. I don't think I asked him where or when.

"In the movies." He laid his head on the fence. "It wasn't really her. It was a woman named Kay Francis. She's a white movie star who looks just like Mother Dear."

There was no difficulty believing that a white movie star looked like our mother and that Bailey had seen her. He told me that the movies changed each week, but when another picture came starring Kay Francis, we'd go together. He even promised to sit with me.

We had to wait almost two months before Kay Francis returned to Stamps. Bailey's mood had improved a lot, but the expectation made him more nervous than he was usually. When he told me that the movie would be shown, we used our best behavior and were the perfect children that Grandmother deserved and wished to think we were.

It was a comedy. The whitefolks downstairs laughed every few minutes. The sound would remain in the air for a second before the people in the balcony accepted it and sent their own laughter to join with it.

I laughed, too, but not at the hateful jokes made about my people. I laughed because, except that she was white, the big movie star looked just like my mother. Except that she lived in a big house with a thousand servants, she lived just like my mother. And it was funny to think the whitefolks didn't know that the woman they were admiring could be my mother's twin, except that she was white and my mother was prettier. Much prettier.

The movie star made me happy. It was extraordinary good fortune to be able to save one's money and go to see one's mother whenever one wanted to. I left the theater feeling as if I'd been given an unexpected present. But Bailey was depressed again. (I had to beg him not to stay for the next show.) On the way home he stopped at the railroad track and waited for the night train. Just before it reached the crossing, he jumped out and ran across the tracks.

I was left on the other side going crazy. Maybe the huge wheels had killed him. Or even worse, maybe he caught the train and was gone for ever.

When the train passed he pushed himself away from the pole where he had been leaning, laughed at me for making all that noise, and said, "Let's go home."

One year later he did catch a train, but he didn't find his Mother Dear—he got stuck in Baton Rouge, Louisiana, for two weeks.

♦

The summer picnic fish fry by the lake was the biggest outdoor event of the year. Everyone was there. All churches were represented, as well as the social groups, professional people (Negro teachers from Lafayette County), and all the excited children.

I had wanted to bring something to read, but Momma said if I didn't want to play with the other children I could make myself useful by cleaning fish or bringing water from the nearest well. I wandered into a hidden quiet spot by accident. Signs with arrows pointed MEN, WOMEN, CHILDREN toward lanes that were hard to find, grown over since last year. Feeling old and very wise at ten, I couldn't allow myself to be found by the small children peeing behind a tree. Nor did I dare to follow the arrow pointing the way for WOMEN. So when I needed to pee, I headed in another direction. When I got through the wall of trees I found myself in an open space much smaller than the picnic area, and cool and quiet. After my business was taken care of, I found a seat and leaned back on a tree trunk. This is what

Heaven would be like. Maybe California, too. Looking straight up at the sky, I felt far away.

There was a sound of footsteps on the grass and I jumped at being found. I didn't know that she too was escaping the noise of the picnic. We were the same age, and she and her mother lived in a neat little house behind the school. Her cousins, who were our age, were wealthier and lighter-skinned, but I had secretly believed that Louise was the prettiest female in Stamps, after Mrs. Flowers.

"What are you doing here by yourself, Marguerite?" She didn't accuse, she asked for information. I said that I was watching the sky. She asked, "What for?" There was obviously no answer to a question like that, so I didn't make up one.

Louise was a lonely girl, although she had plenty of playmates and was always ready to be a partner for any game in the schoolyard. Her face, which was long and dark chocolate brown, was sad. And her eyes, which I thought were her best feature, shifted quickly as if what they sought had just a second before escaped her.

She had come near and the light through the trees shined on her face and hair. I had never noticed before, but she looked exactly like Bailey. Her hair was "good"—more straight than kinky—and her features were perfect.

She looked up—"Well, you can't see much sky from here." Then she sat down, an arm's length away from me. Slowly she leaned against the tree. I closed my eyes and thought about finding another place, but I realized that there probably wasn't another as good as this one. There was a little scream and before I could open my eyes, Louise had grabbed my hand. "I was falling"—she shook her long hair—"I was falling in the sky."

I liked her for being able to fall in the sky and admit it. I suggested, "Let's try it together. But we have to sit up straight

54

after counting to five." Louise asked, "Want to hold hands? Just in case?" I did. If one of us did fall, the other could pull her out.

After a few near-falls, we laughed at having played with death and escaped.

Louise said, "Let's look at the sky while we're spinning." We took each other's hands in the center of the open space and began turning around. Very slowly at first. We raised our chins and looked straight up at the patch of blue. Faster, just a little faster, then faster, and even faster. Yes, help, we were falling. We couldn't stop spinning or falling until I fell out of her grasp and was thrown down. I found myself safe at the foot of the tree. Louise had landed on her knees at the other side of the open space.

This was surely the time to laugh. First we were giggling and crawling toward each other and then we were laughing out loud crazily. We hit each other on the back and shoulders and laughed some more.

By daring to challenge the unknown with me, she became my first friend. We spent many hours teaching ourselves a secret language. This made us superior to other children. At last I began to understand what girls giggled about. Louise would say a few sentences to me in our secret language and would laugh. Of course, I laughed too. After all, girls have to giggle. After being a woman for three years, I became a girl.

◆

In school one day, a girl I hardly knew and had scarcely spoken to brought me a note. The way it was folded indicated that it was a love note. I was sure she had the wrong person, but she insisted. I confessed to myself that I was frightened. Suppose it was somebody being funny? Fortunately I had got permission to go to the toilet—outside—and in the darkness I read:

55

Dear Friend, M.J.
Times are hard and friends are few
I take great pleasure in writing you
Will you be my valentine?
Tommy Valdon

I struggled to remember. Who? Who was Tommy Valdon? Finally a face dragged itself from my memory. He was the nice-looking brown-skinned boy who lived across the lake. As soon as I realized that, I began to wonder: Why? Why me? Was it a joke? But if Tommy was the boy I remembered he was a serious person and a good student. Well, then it wasn't a joke. All right, what evil, dirty things did he have in mind? What did a valentine do, anyway?

I thought of Louise. I could show it to her. I folded the paper and went back to class. After classes I waited for her. She was talking to a group of girls, laughing. But when I gave her our special signal (two waves of the left hand) she said goodbye to them and joined me in the road. I didn't give her the chance to ask what was on my mind (her favorite question); I just gave her the note. Recognizing the way it was folded she stopped smiling. She opened the letter and read it aloud twice. "Well, looks like he wants you to be his valentine."

"Louise, I can read. But what does it mean?"

"Oh, you know. His valentine. His love."

There was that hateful word again.

"Well, I won't. I certainly won't. Not ever again."

"Have you been his valentine before? What do you mean never again?"

I couldn't lie to my friend and I wasn't going to bring back bad memories.

"Well, don't answer him then, and that's the end of it." I was glad that she thought it could be gotten rid of so quickly. I tore the note in half and gave her a part. Walking down the hill we tore the paper into a thousand pieces and gave it to the wind.

Two days later an eighth grader came into my classroom. She spoke quietly to Miss Williams, our teacher. Miss Williams said, "Class, I believe you remember that tomorrow is Valentine's Day. The day is observed by exchanging cards. The eighth grade children have completed theirs and this girl is acting as mailman. Now, stand when your name is called."

We who were being called to receive valentines were only slightly more embarrassed than those who sat and watched as Miss Williams opened each envelope and read the message aloud. I was filled with shame and anticipation but had time to be offended at the silly poetry.

"Marguerite Anne Johnson. This looks more like a letter than a valentine. 'Dear Friend, I wrote you a letter and saw you tear it up with your friend Miss L. I don't believe you meant to hurt my feelings, so whether you answer or not you will always be my valentine. T.V.'"

"Class"—Miss Williams grinned and continued—"although you are only in seventh grade, I'm sure you wouldn't be so impudent as to sign a letter with your initials. But here is a boy in the eighth grade, who will soon graduate ... You may collect your valentines and these letters on your way out."

It was a nice letter and Tommy had beautiful handwriting. I was sorry I tore up the first. I felt good about his statement that his feelings would not be influenced by whether I answered him or not. He couldn't be wanting you-know-what if he talked like that. I told Louise that the next time he came to the Store I was going to say something extra nice to him. Unfortunately the situation was so wonderful to me that each time I saw Tommy I giggled uncontrollably and was unable to form a complete sentence. After a while he stopped including me in his general glances.

57

Chapter 10   Graduation

The children in Stamps trembled visibly with anticipation. Some adults were excited too. Large classes were graduating from both the elementary school and the high school. Even those who were years away from their own graduation were anxious to help with preparations as a kind of practice.

Parents who could afford it had ordered new shoes and ready-made clothes for themselves. They also hired the women who did the best sewing to make graduation dresses and cut down secondhand pants for the important event.

Oh, it was certainly important. Whitefolks would attend the ceremony, and two or three would speak of God and home, and the Southern way of life. The principal's wife would play the graduation march while the lower-grade graduates walked to their seats below the platform. The high school seniors would wait in empty classrooms to make their dramatic entrance.

In the Store I was the person of the moment. Bailey had graduated the year before. My class was wearing yellow dresses, and Momma had put special effort into mine. I was going to be beautiful—a model of fine hand-sewing. It didn't worry me that I was only twelve years old and was just graduating from eighth grade.

I had started smiling more often, and my jaws hurt from the new activity. As a member of the winning team (the graduating class of 1940) I had put unpleasant feelings behind me. I was heading for freedom.

My work had earned me a top place in my class and I was going to be one of the first called in the graduating ceremonies. No absences, no late arrivals, and my academic work was among the best of the year.

My hair pleased me too. Gradually the black mass had lengthened and thickened, so that at last it stayed in its place and didn't hurt my head when I tried to comb it.

Among Negroes the tradition was to give presents to children going only from one grade to another. How much more important this was when the person was graduating at the top of the class. Uncle Willie and Momma had sent away for a Mickey Mouse watch like Bailey's. Louise gave me four handkerchiefs with hand-sewn designs. Mrs. Sneed, the minister's wife, made me an underskirt to wear for graduation, and nearly every customer gave me a nickel or even a dime with the instruction "Keep on moving to higher ground," or similar encouragement.

Amazingly the great day finally dawned and I was out of bed before I knew it. I threw open the back door to see it more clearly. I hoped the memory of that morning would never leave me. Barefoot in the backyard, I enjoyed the gentle warmth and thanked God that no matter what evil I had done in my life, He had allowed me to live to see this day.

Bailey came out and gave me a box wrapped in Christmas paper. He said he had saved his money for months to pay for it. He was as proud of the gift as I was. It was a soft-leather copy of a collection of poems by Edgar Allen Poe. I turned to "Annabel Lee," my favorite, and we walked up and down the garden rows reading the beautiful lines.

Momma made a Sunday breakfast although it was only Friday. After we finished the prayers, I opened my eyes to find the watch on my plate. It was a dream of a day. Everything went smoothly, and I didn't have to be reminded of anything. Near evening I was too nervous to do my chores, so Bailey volunteered to do them all before his bath.

Days before, we had made a sign for the Store, and as we turned out the lights, Momma hung it over the door handle. It read clearly: CLOSED. GRADUATION.

My dress fitted perfectly and everyone said that I looked like a sunbeam in it. On the hill, going toward the school, Bailey walked behind with Uncle Willie, who wanted him to walk ahead with us because it embarrassed him to have to walk so slowly. Bailey said he'd let the ladies walk together, and the men would follow. We all laughed, nicely.

The other members of my graduating class were standing around the front steps. I joined them and didn't even see my family go in to find seats in the crowded room. The school band played a march and all the classes walked in as we had practiced. We stood in front of our seats until the principal signaled to us to take our seats. As I sat down, I was overcome with a feeling that something unplanned was going to happen, and we were going to be made to look bad.

The principal welcomed "parents and friends" and asked the Baptist minister to lead us in prayer. When the principal spoke again, his voice had changed; it was weak and uncertain. He talked about Booker T. Washington,★ our "great leader." Then he said a few things about friendship and the friendship of kind-hearted people to those less fortunate than themselves. His voice could hardly be heard. When he finished, he paused and then said clearly, "Our speaker tonight, who is also our friend, came from Texarkana to deliver the graduation speech, but due to the irregularity of the train schedule, he's going to, as they say, 'speak and run.'" He said that we understood and wanted the man to know that we were most grateful for the time he was able to give us. Then he introduced Mr. Edward Donleavy.

Not one but two white men came through the door at the side of the stage. The shorter one walked to the speaker's platform and the tall one sat down in the principal's seat. The Baptist minister gave the principal his chair and walked off the stage.

Donleavy looked at the audience once (I'm sure that he only wanted to confirm that we were really there), adjusted his glasses, and began to read from a pile of papers.

★ Booker T. Washington: a nineteenth-century Black educator

He was glad "to be here and to see the work going on just as it was in the other schools." He told us of the wonderful changes we children in Stamps would see. The Central School (naturally, the white school was Central) had already been granted improvements that would be in use in the fall. A well-known artist was coming from Little Rock to teach art to them. They were going to have the newest equipment in their science laboratory. Mr. Donleavy made sure we knew who made these improvements available to Central High and said that we wouldn't be ignored in the general improvement plan he had in mind.

He said that he had pointed out to people at a very high level that one of the first-line football players at Arkansas Agricultural and Mechanical College had graduated from Lafayette County Training School. He went on to say how proud he was that "one of the best basketball players at Fisk University sank his first ball right here at Lafayette County Training School."

The white kids were going to have a chance to become Galileos and Madame Curies and Edisons and Gauguins, and our boys (the girls weren't even included) would try to be Jesse Owenses and Joe Louises.*

Owens and Louis were great Black heroes, but what school official in the white-kingdom of Little Rock had the right to decide that those two men must be our only heroes?

The man's words brought silence to the room. Held back by hard-learned manners, I couldn't look behind me, but to my left and right the proud graduating class of 1940 had dropped their heads. Every girl in my row had found something new to do with her handkerchief.

Graduation, the magic time of gifts and congratulations and diplomas, was finished for me before my name was called. The

* Jesse Owens and Joe Louis: Jesse Owens was a Black runner, winner of many races. Joe Louis was a Black champion fighter.

achievement was for nothing. All our learning was for nothing. Donleavy had shown us who we were.

We were servants, farmers, and washer-women. Anything higher that we dreamed about was ridiculous.

It was awful to be Negro and have no control over my life. It was terrible to be young and already trained to sit quietly and listen to charges brought against my color with no chance of defense. We should all be dead.

Donleavy was running for election, and assured our parents that if he won we would have the only cement playing field for colored people in that part of Arkansas. Also, we were sure to get new equipment for cooking, sewing, and woodworking classes.

He finished, nodded to the men on the stage, and the tall man who was never introduced joined him at the door. They left with the attitude that now they were going to something really important.

The ugliness they left could be felt in the air. My name had lost its familiarity and I had to be gently pushed to go and receive my diploma. All my preparations were forgotten. I neither marched up to the stage like a confident winner, nor did I look in the audience for Bailey's nod of approval. Marguerite Johnson, I heard the name again. My honors were read, there were noises of appreciation in the audience, and I took my place on the stage as practiced.

Then Henry Reed, our top graduate, was giving his speech, "To Be or Not to Be." Hadn't he heard the whitefolks? We couldn't *be*, so the question was a waste of time. The world didn't think we had minds, and they let us know it. I was amazed that Henry could give the speech as if we had a choice.

I had been listening with my eyes closed and silently proving false each sentence; then there was a silence, which in an audience warns that something unplanned is happening. I looked up and saw Henry Reed, the perfectly-behaved boy, the A student, turn his back to the audience and turn to us (the proud graduating class of 1940) and sing, nearly speaking,

"Lift every voice and sing ..."

It was the poem written by James Weldon Johnson. It was the music written by J. Rosamond Johnson. It was the Negro national anthem. We were singing it out of habit.

Our mothers and fathers stood in the dark hall and joined the song of encouragement. Every child I knew had learned that song with the alphabet. But I personally had never heard it before. Never heard the words, despite the thousands of times I had sung them. Never thought they had anything to do with me. Now I heard, really heard it, for the first time.

While echoes of the song hung in the air, Henry Reed bowed his head, said "Thank you," and returned to his place in the line. The tears that slipped down many faces were not wiped away in shame.

We were on top again. As always, again. We survived. I was no longer only a member of the proud graduating class of 1940; I was a proud member of the wonderful, beautiful Negro race.

Chapter 11   California

Momma told us one day that she was taking us to California. She explained that we were growing up, that we needed to be with our parents, that Uncle Willie was crippled, that she was getting too old. All true, but none of those truths satisfied our need for The Truth. The Store and the rooms in back became a going-away factory. Momma sat at the sewing machine for hours, making and remaking clothes for use in California.

Whatever the real reason, The Truth, for taking us to California, I shall always think it lay mostly in an incident in which Bailey had the leading part. On an afternoon a few weeks before Momma revealed her plan to take us West, Bailey came into the Store shaking. His face was no longer black but a dirty, colorless gray. As we always did when we entered the Store, he walked behind the candy counter and leaned on the cash register. Uncle Willie had sent him on an errand to whitefolks' town and he wanted an explanation for Bailey's late return. After a brief moment our uncle could see that something was wrong and, feeling unable to cope, he called Momma from the kitchen.

"What's the matter, Bailey Junior?"

He said nothing. I knew when I saw him that it would be useless to ask anything while he was in that state. It meant that he had seen or heard of something so ugly or frightening that he couldn't make himself respond as a result. He had explained when we were young that when things were very bad his soul went to sleep. When it awoke, the fearful thing had gone away. I had to swear that when his soul was sleeping, I would never try to wake it; the shock might make it go to sleep for ever. So I left him alone, and after a while Momma had to leave him alone too.

When he felt better he asked Uncle Willie what colored people had done to white people to make them hate us. Uncle Willie, who was not used to explaining things because he was like Momma, said little except that "colored people hadn't even bothered a hair on whitefolks' heads."

Bailey said he saw a man, a colored man, who was dead.

Uncle Willie asked, "Who—who was it?"

Bailey said, "When I passed the prison, some men had just fished him out of the lake. He was wrapped in a sheet, all rolled up. Then a white man walked over and pulled the sheet off. The man was on his back but the white man stuck his foot under the sheet and rolled him over on his stomach. He had no color at all, and he was blown up like a ball. The colored men backed away, and I did, too, but the white man stood there, looking down, and grinned. Uncle Willie, why do they hate us so much?"

Uncle Willie replied, "They don't really hate us. They don't know us. How can they hate us? They're mostly scared."

Momma asked if Bailey had recognized the man, but he didn't hear her.

"Mr. Bubba told me I was too young to see something like that and I ought to go straight home, but I had to stay. Then the white man called us closer. He said, 'O.K., you boys, take him into the prison. When the Sheriff comes, he'll inform his family. This is one nigger nobody has to worry about anymore. He ain't going nowhere else.' Then the men picked up corners of the sheet, but since nobody wanted to get close to the man they held only the ends, and he almost rolled out on the ground. The white man called me to come and help too."

Momma exploded. "Who was it?" She made herself clear. "Who was the white man?"

Bailey couldn't let go of the horror. "I picked up a side of the sheet and walked in the prison with the men. I walked in the prison carrying a rotten dead Negro." His voice was ancient with shock. His eyes were huge.

"The white man pretended he was going to lock us all in there, but Mr. Bubba said, 'Oh, Mr. Jim. We didn't do it. We ain't done nothing wrong.' Then the white man laughed and said we boys couldn't take a joke, and opened the door." He breathed his relief. "I was glad to get out of there. The prison, and the prisoners screaming that they didn't want any dead nigger in there with them. That he'd make the place smell bad. They called the white man 'Boss.' They said, 'Boss, surely we ain't done nothing bad enough for you to put another nigger in here with us, and a dead one, too.' Then they laughed. They all laughed like there was something funny."

Bailey was talking so fast he forgot to stutter. He was thinking

65

about a mystery that young Southern Black boys start to solve, *try* to solve, from the time they're seven years old until their death. The humorless puzzle of inequality and hate. His experience raised the question of worth and values, of aggressive inferiority and aggressive arrogance. Could Uncle Willie, a Black man, Southern, and crippled, hope to answer the questions, asked and unasked? Would Momma, who knew the ways of the whites and the ways of the Blacks, try to answer her grandson, whose life depended on him not truly understanding the mystery? Most certainly not.

They both responded characteristically. Uncle Willie said something like he didn't know what the world was coming to, and Momma prayed, "God rest his soul, poor man." I'm sure she began planning the details of our California trip that night.

♦

Our transportation was Momma's major concern for many weeks. She had arranged with a railroad employee to provide her with a pass in exchange for groceries. The pass allowed a reduced fare only, and even that had to be approved. So we had to wait until white people we would never see, in offices we would never visit, signed and stamped and mailed the pass back to Momma. My fare had to be paid in cash. Taking that much money out of our cash register was financially difficult. Momma decided Bailey couldn't accompany us, but that he would follow within a month or so when the bills were paid. Although our mother now lived in San Francisco, Momma must have felt it wiser to go first to Los Angeles, where our father was. She had me write letters, telling me what to write, advising them both that we were on our way.

And we were on our way, but unable to say when. Our clothes were washed, ironed, and packed. Neighbors, who understood the difficulties of travel, said goodbye a million times. A widowed friend of Momma's had agreed to take care of Uncle Willie. After thousands of false departures, at last we left Stamps.

My sorrow was limited to sadness at separating from Bailey for a month (we had never been separated), the imagined loneliness of Uncle Willie (at thirty-five, he'd never been separated from his mother), and the loss of Louise, my first friend. I wouldn't miss Mrs. Flowers, because she had given me her secret word which would help me all my life: books.

I didn't actually think about meeting Mother until the last day of our journey. I was "going to California." To oranges and sunshine and movie stars and earthquakes and (finally I realized) to Mother. My old guilt returned. I wondered if Mr. Freeman's name would be mentioned, or if I would be expected to say something about the situation myself. I certainly couldn't ask Momma, and Bailey was a million miles away.

I was unprepared to meet my mother. Too soon she stood before me, smaller than I remembered but more wonderful than any memory. She wore a light-brown suit, shoes to match, and a hat with a feather in the band. She patted my face with her gloved hands. She kissed and laughed and rushed about collecting our coats and organizing our luggage. She easily took care of the details. I was amazed again at how wonderful she was.

We moved into an apartment, and I slept on a sofa that was changed at night into a large comfortable bed. Mother stayed in Los Angeles long enough to get us settled. Then she returned to San Francisco to find a place to live for her suddenly larger family.

Momma and Bailey (he joined us a month after our arrival) and I lived in Los Angeles for about six months while our permanent living arrangements were being finalized. Daddy Bailey visited occasionally, bringing shopping bags of fruit. He was like a Sun God, bringing warmth and light to our lives.

When the arrangements for our move north were completed,

Momma gave us the shocking news that she was going back to Arkansas. She had done her job. She was needed by Uncle Willie. We had our own parents at last. At least we were all in the same state.

There were days of unknowing for Bailey and me. It was fine to say that we would be with our parents, but who were they? Would they be more severe with our mistakes than she? That would be bad. Or less severe? That would be even worse. Would we learn to speak the fast language of our Mexican neighbors? I doubted that, and I doubted even more that I would ever find out what they laughed about so loudly and so often.

I would have been willing to return to Stamps even without Bailey. But Momma left for Arkansas without me.

Mother drove us toward San Francisco over the big white highway that seemed like it would never end. She talked constantly and pointed out places of interest. She told humorous stories and tried to win our attention. But her personality, and the fact that she was our mother, had done the job so successfully that her efforts were unnecessary. Nothing could have been more magical than to have found her at last, and have her completely to ourselves in the closed world of a moving car.

Although we were both delighted, Bailey and I were aware of her nervousness. The knowledge that we had the power to upset that godlike person made us look at each other and smile. It also made her human.

We spent a few months in an Oakland apartment which had a bathtub in the kitchen and was near enough to the train station to shake at the arrival and departure of every train. In many ways it was like being in St. Louis again—and Grandma Baxter was again living with us.

We went to school and no family member questioned the amount or quality of our work. We went to a playground which had a basketball court, a football field, and table tennis tables in shelters with roofs. On Sundays, instead of going to church, we went to the movies.

I slept with Grandmother Baxter. One evening after going to bed normally, I was awakened by a shaking. I saw my mother kneeling by my bed. She brought her face close to my ear.

"Ritie," she whispered, "Ritie. Come, but be very quiet." Then she quietly rose and left the room. Dutifully, I followed. The light coming through the half-opened kitchen door showed Bailey's pajamaed legs hanging from the covered bathtub. The clock on the dining-room table said 2:30. I had never been up at that hour.

I looked questioningly at Bailey and knew by his response that there was nothing to fear. Then I quickly thought about the list of important events. It wasn't anybody's birthday, or April Fool's Day, or Halloween, but it was something.

Mother closed the kitchen door and told me to sit beside Bailey. She put her hands on her waist and said we had been invited to a party.

Was that why she woke us in the middle of the night! Neither of us said anything.

She continued, "I am giving a party and you are my honored and only guests."

She opened the oven and took out a pan of her cookies and showed us a pot of chocolate milk on the back of the stove. We could only laugh at our beautiful and wild mother. When Bailey and I started laughing, she joined in, but she kept her finger in front of her mouth to try to quiet us.

We were served formally, and she apologized for not having a band to play for us but said she'd sing instead. She sang and danced. What child can resist a mother who laughs freely and often, especially if the child is mature enough to understand the joke?

◆

World War II started on a Sunday afternoon when I was on my way to the movies. People in the streets shouted, "We're at war. We've declared war on Japan."

I ran all the way home, unsure whether I would be bombed before I reached Bailey and Mother. Grandmother Baxter calmed my anxiety by explaining that America would not be bombed, not as long as Franklin Delano Roosevelt was president. He knew what he was doing.

Soon after, Mother married Daddy Clidell, who became the first father I would know. He was a successful businessman, and he and Mother moved us to San Francisco. Grandmother remained in the big house in Oakland.

◆

In the early months of World War II, San Francisco's Fillmore district experienced a visible change. The Asian population disappeared. As the Japanese left, soundlessly and without protest, the Negroes entered. Japanese shops were taken over by Negro businessmen, and in less than a year became permanent homes for the newly arrived Southern Blacks. No member of my family and none of the family friends ever mentioned the absent Japanese. It was as if they had never owned or lived in the houses that were now ours.

The sense of change, the lack of permanence of life in wartime, and the awkward behavior of the recent arrivals helped to lessen my own sense of not belonging. In San Francisco, for the first time, I saw myself as part of something. I didn't identify with the newcomers, nor with the Black natives of San Francisco, nor with the whites or even the Asians. I identified with the times and the city. The feeling of fear that San Francisco would be bombed strengthened my sense of belonging. Hadn't I always thought that life was just one great risk?

To me, a thirteen-year-old Black girl, used to the South and

Southern Black lifestyle, the city was a state of beauty and a state of freedom. I became free of fears. Feeling safe, I was certain that no one loved San Francisco as I did.

Chapter 12   Education

Although my grades were very good (I had been put up two semesters on my arrival from Stamps), I was unable to settle down in the high school. It was an institution for girls near my house, and the young ladies were faster, meaner, and more prejudiced than any I had met at Lafayette County Training School. Many of the Negro girls were, like me, from the South, but they had lived in—or claimed to have lived in—the big cities. They walked like they couldn't be beaten by anyone, and they frightened the white girls and those Black students who weren't protected by fearlessness. Fortunately I was transferred to George Washington High School.

The buildings sat on a moderate hill in the white residential district, about sixty blocks from the Negro neighborhood. For the first semester, I was one of three Black students in the school, and in that special situation I learned to love my people more. In the mornings as the streetcar left my neighborhood I experienced a mixture of fear and anxiety. I knew that soon we would be out of my familiar setting and Blacks who were on the streetcar when I got on would all be gone. I alone would face the forty blocks of neat streets, white houses, and rich children.

In the evenings on the way home I felt joy, anticipation, and relief when I saw the first brown faces on the streets. I recognized that I was again in my country.

In the school I was disappointed to find out that I was not the most intelligent or even nearly the most intelligent student. The white kids had better vocabularies than I and had less fear in the

71

classrooms. They never hesitated to hold up their hands in response to a teacher's question; even when they were wrong they were wrong aggressively, while I had to be certain about all my facts before I dared to call attention to myself.

George Washington High School was the first real school I attended. My entire time there might have been time lost if it hadn't been for the unique personality of a wonderful teacher. Miss Kirwin was that rare educator who was in love with information. I will always believe that her love of teaching came not only from her liking for students but also from her desire to make sure that some of the things she knew would find new places to be stored so that they could be shared again.

Miss Kirwin greeted each class with "Good day, ladies and gentlemen." I had never heard an adult speak with such respect to teenagers. (Adults usually believe that a show of honor lessens their authority.) "In today's *Chronicle* there was an article on the mining industry in the Carolinas [or some subject about a distant place]. I am certain that all of you have read the article. I would like someone to explain the subject for me."

After the first two weeks in her class I, and all the other excited students, read the San Francisco papers, *Time* magazine, *Life* magazine, and everything else available to us.

Miss Kirwin encouraged us instead of threatening us. While some of the other teachers made an effort to be nice to me—to be a "liberal" with me—and others ignored me completely, Miss Kirwin never seemed to notice that I was Black and therefore different. I was Miss Johnson, and if I had the answer to a question she asked I was never given anymore than the word "Correct," which was what she said to every other student with the correct answer.

Years later when I returned to San Francisco, I visited her classroom. She always remembered that I was Miss Johnson, who had a good mind and should be doing something with it. I was

72

never encouraged on those visits to stay long. She acted as if I must have had other visits to make. I often wondered if she knew she was the only teacher I remember.

♦

I never knew why I was given a free place to the California Labor School. It was a college for adults. At fourteen I accepted a free place and got one for the next year as well. So in the evenings I took drama and dance classes, with white and Black grownups. My days centered around Miss Kirwin's class, dinner with Bailey and Mother, and drama and dance.

The people I was loyal to at this time in my life were a strange combination: Momma with her determination, Mrs. Flowers and her books, Bailey with his love, my mother and her happiness, Miss Kirwin and her information, my evening classes of drama and dance.

♦

I was prepared to accept Daddy Clidell as one more faceless name added to Mother's list of men. I had trained myself so successfully through the years to display interest, or at least attention, while my mind wandered freely on other subjects, that I could have lived in his house without ever seeing him and without him being aware of my behavior. But his character encouraged admiration. He was a simple man who didn't feel inferior about his lack of education and, even more amazing, showed no superiority because he had succeeded despite that lack.

He owned apartment buildings, and was famous for being that rarity, "a man of honor." Unexpectedly, I looked like him, and when he, Mother, and I walked down the street his friends often said, "Clidell, that's sure your daughter. Ain't no way you can deny her."

73

Proud laughter followed those declarations, since he had never had children. Because of his late-arriving but strong sense of fatherhood, I was introduced to the most colorful characters in the Black community. Daddy Clidell explained to me that they were the most successful con men in the world, and they were going to tell me about some games so that I would never be "anybody's mark."

Then they took turns showing me their tricks, how they chose their victims ("marks") from the wealthy prejudiced whites, and how they used the victims' prejudice against them.

Some of the stories were funny, a few were sad, but all were amusing or satisfying to me. The Black man, the con man who could act the most stupid, won every time over the powerful, arrogant white. My favorite story was about two Black men who conned a white man into paying them $40,000 for a piece of land in Oklahoma. The land wasn't theirs; it really belonged to the state. Those storytellers, born Black and male before the turn of the twentieth century, should have been failures. Instead they used their intelligence to force open the door of rejection and not only became wealthy but got some revenge, too.

It wasn't possible for me to regard them as criminals; I was proud of their achievements.

♦

My education and that of my Black friends were quite different from the education of our white schoolmates. In the classroom we all learned verb tenses, but in the streets and in our homes the Blacks learned to drop "*s*"s from plurals and endings from past-tense verbs. We were aware of the gap separating the written word from the spoken. We learned to change from one language to another without being conscious of the effort. At school, we might respond with "That's not unusual." But in the street, in the same situation, we easily said, "It be's like that sometimes."

Chapter 13   A Vacation

I was going on a vacation. Daddy Bailey invited me to spend the summer with him in southern California and I was nervous with excitement. Since our father's characteristic attitude was one of superiority, I secretly expected him to live in a huge house surrounded by a large yard and serviced by a paid staff.

Daddy Bailey had a girlfriend, who had begun writing letters to me some months before, and she would meet me at the train. We had agreed to wear white flowers to identify ourselves. On the platform I saw a little girl who wore a white flower, but dismissed her as improbable. The platform emptied as we walked by each other time after time. Finally she stopped me with a disbelieving "Marguerite?" Her voice sounded shocked and mature. So, she wasn't a little girl. I, too, was surprised.

She said, "I'm Dolores Stockland."

Shocked but trying to sound well mannered, I said, "Hello. My name is Marguerite."

Daddy's girlfriend? I guessed that she was in her early twenties. Her suit, shoes, and gloves informed me that she was well-dressed and serious. I thought that if she was planning to marry our father she must have been scared to find that his daughter was nearly six feet tall and not even pretty. (I found out later that Daddy Bailey had told her that his children were eight and nine years old and good-looking.)

I was another link in a long chain of disappointments. Daddy had promised to marry her but kept delaying until he finally married another woman. Instead of owning a huge house and servants, Daddy lived in a small house on the outskirts of town. Dolores lived there with him and kept the house clean and orderly. She loved him, and her life would have been perfect. And then I arrived.

She tried hard to make me into something she could

75

reasonably accept. Her first attempt, which failed completely, concerned my attention to details. I was asked, begged, then ordered to take care of my room. My willingness to do so was made difficult by my ignorance of how it should be done and my awkwardness with small objects. The dresser in my room was covered with little breakable objects. If and when I remembered to dust them, I always held one too tightly and broke off a leg or two, or too loosely and dropped it, and it broke into pieces.

Dad spoke Spanish well, and since I had studied for a year, we were able to have short conversations. I believe that my talent with a foreign language was the only quality I had that impressed Dolores. She couldn't attempt the strange sounds. Admittedly, though, her English, like everything else about her, was absolutely perfect.

We had a test of strength for weeks as Dad watched, not getting involved but greatly enjoying himself. He was amused and seemed to enjoy our discomfort. He asked me once if I "liked my mother." I thought he meant my mother, so I answered yes—she was beautiful and happy and very kind. He said he wasn't talking about Vivian; he meant Dolores. Then I explained that I didn't like her because she was mean. He laughed. When I added that she didn't like me because I was tall and arrogant and wasn't clean enough for her, he laughed harder and said something like, "Well, that's life."

One evening he announced that on the next day he was going to Mexico to buy food for the weekend. There was nothing unusual about his announcement until he added that he was taking me along. He filled the shocked silence with the information that a trip to Mexico would give me an opportunity to practice Spanish.

Dolores' silence might have been the result of a jealous reaction, but mine was caused by total surprise. My father had not shown any particular pride in me and very little love. He had not taken me to his friends or to southern California's few points of interest. It was unbelievable that I was being included in something as exciting as a trip to Mexico. Well, I quickly reasoned, I deserved it. I was his daughter, and my vacation wasn't what I had expected a vacation to be.

In the morning, we started on the foreign adventure. The dirt roads of Mexico satisfied my desire for an unusual experience. Dad gave no explanation as we drove through the border town and headed for the interior. After a few miles we were stopped by a uniformed guard. He and Dad exchanged familiar greetings and Dad got out of the car. He reached back into the pocket on the door and took a bottle of alcohol into the guard's kiosk. They laughed and talked for over a half hour as I sat in the car and tried to translate the quiet sounds. Eventually they came out and walked to the car. Dad still had the bottle but it was only half full. He asked the guard if he would like to marry me. At once the guard leaned into the car and patted my cheek. He told Dad that he would marry me and we would have "many babies." My father thought that was the funniest thing he had heard since we left home. After many *adiós*es★ Dad started the car, and we were on our way again.

Signs informed me that we were heading for Ensenada. On that journey along the twisted roads beside the steep mountain, I feared that I would never get back to America, civilization, English, and wide streets again. Our destination was, in fact, not the town of Ensenada, but a place about five miles out of the city limits. We pulled up in the dirt yard of a *cantina*, where half-clothed children chased mean-looking chickens around and around. The noise of the car brought women to the door of the old building.

A woman's voice sang out, "Bailey, Bailey." And suddenly a group of women crowded to the door and overflowed into the

★ *adiós*: Spanish for "good-bye"; other Spanish words and phrases are *cantina* (small bar), la *niña de Bailey* (Bailey's daughter), *señoritas* (young women), *Pasa* (Pass), *¿Quién es?* (Who is it?), *mi padre* (my father), *¿Qué pasa?* (What's happening?), and *¿Qué quiere?* (What do you want?)

yard. Dad told me to get out of the car, and we went to meet the women. He explained quickly that I was his daughter, which everyone thought was uncontrollably funny. We were taken into a large room with a bar at one end. There were a few men sitting at the bar, and they greeted my father with relaxed familiarity. I was taken around and each person was told my name and age. People patted me on the back, shook Dad's hand, and spoke a rapid Spanish that I was unable to follow. Bailey was the hero of the hour, and as he responded to the open show of friendship I saw a new side of the man.

It seemed hard to believe that he was a lonely person, searching in bottles of alcohol, under women's skirts, in church work and important job titles for his "personal place," lost before birth and never recovered. It was obvious to me then that he had never belonged in Stamps, and belonged even less to the slow-moving, slow-thinking Johnson family.

In the Mexican bar Dad was relaxed, which I had never seen before. There was no need to pretend in front of those poor Mexican farmers. As he was, just being himself, he was impressive enough to them. He was an American. He was Black. He spoke Spanish well. He had money and he could drink alcohol with the best of them. The women liked him too. He was tall and handsome and generous.

It was a party. Someone put on music, and drinks were served to all the customers. I was given a warm Coca-Cola. I was asked to dance. I hesitated because I wasn't sure I'd be able to follow the steps, but Dad nodded and encouraged me to try. I had been enjoying myself for at least an hour before I realized it. I was happy, Dad was proud, and my new friends were pleasant. I ate, danced, screamed, and drank the extra-sweet and sticky Coca-Cola. As newcomers joined the celebration I was introduced as *la niña de Bailey*, and was quickly accepted.

As the sun went down, I realized that I hadn't seen my father for a long time. When the dance finished, I made my way through the crowd of people. I was frightened. He wasn't in the room. Had he made an arrangement with the guard back at the pass? I wouldn't have been surprised. The thought of it made my knees weak. Dad was gone. He was probably halfway back home with the money from selling me in his pocket. I had to get to the door, which seemed a very long distance away.

Seen through the open door, Dad's car looked beautiful. He hadn't left me. I immediately felt better. I decided to sit in his car and wait for him, since he couldn't have gone far. I knew he was with a woman, and the more I thought about it, it was easy to figure which one of the *señoritas* he had taken away. She had been the first to rush to him, and that was when he quickly said, "This is my daughter. She speaks Spanish." If Dolores knew, she would die. The thought of that kept me happy for a long time.

It was getting darker. I began to feel afraid as I considered the possibility of sitting in the car all night alone. I tried to stop the flood of fear. Why was I afraid of the Mexicans? They had been kind to me and surely my father wouldn't allow his daughter to be treated badly. Would he? How could he leave me in that bar and go off with his woman? Did he care what happened to me? Not at all, I decided, and began to cry. I was going to die, after all, in a Mexican dirt yard. I would depart from this life without recognition.

I recognized his shadow in the near-dark and was ready to jump out and run to him when I noticed that he was being supported by a small woman I had seen earlier and a man. They guided him toward the door of the *cantina*. If he got inside we might never leave. I got out of the car and went to them. I asked Dad if he would like to get into the car and rest a little. He recognized me and answered that that was exactly what he wanted; he was a little tired, and he'd like to rest before we left. He told his friends his wishes in Spanish and they led him to the car. When I opened the front door, he said, "No." He'd lie down on the back seat for a little while. We got him into the car and he fell asleep immediately.

I thought fast as the couple laughed and spoke to me in Spanish that I couldn't understand. I had never driven a car before, but I had watched carefully and my mother was declared to be the best driver in San Francisco. *She* declared it, at least. I was extremely intelligent and had good physical skills. Of course I could drive. I asked the Mexican man to turn the car around, again in my wonderful high school Spanish, and it took about fifteen minutes to make myself understood. He got in and headed the car toward the highway. He showed his understanding of the situation by his next action. He left the motor running. I put my foot on the accelerator, moved the gear-shift, and with a loud roar we were out of the yard.

I drove down the mountainside toward Calexico, about fifty miles away. When it became totally dark, I felt around until I finally succeeded in finding the lights. The car slowed down as I concentrated on that search, and the engine stopped. A sound from the back seat told me that Dad had fallen off the seat. I pulled the hand brake and carefully considered my next move. We were headed downhill, so I reasoned that with luck we might roll all the way to Calexico—or at least to the guard. I released the brake and we began rolling down the slope. I also stepped on the accelerator, hoping that action would speed our descent, and the motor started. The car went crazily down the hill. The challenge of controlling it was exciting. It was me, Marguerite, driving the car. As I turned the driving wheel and forced the accelerator to the floor, I was controlling Mexico, and aloneness, and inexperienced youth, and Bailey Johnson, Sr.,★ and death and insecurity.

★ Sr.: short for Senior

Eventually the road became level and we started passing scattered lights on each side of the road. No matter what happened after that, I had won. The car began to slow down but we finally reached the guard's box. I pulled on the hand brake and came to a stop. I had to wait until the guard looked into the car and gave me the signal to continue. He was busy talking to people in a car facing the mountain I had just defeated. When he stood up and shouted "*Pasa*," I was surprised. I released the brake, put my foot on the accelerator too quickly. The car leaped left as well as forward and went into the side of the car just leaving. The crash of metal was followed immediately by Spanish shouting from all directions. Strengthened by the excitement that had flooded my brain as we came down the mountainside, I had never felt better. I got out of the car.

The family, eight or more people of every age and size, walked around me, talking excitedly. Someone got the idea to look into the car, and a scream stopped us all. People—there seemed to be hundreds—crowded to the windows and there were more screams. I thought for a minute that something awful might have happened, but then I remembered the sounds of my father sleeping. The family came back, this time not as close but more threatening. When I was able to understand one question, "*¿Quién es?*" I answered without concern, "*Mi padre.*" Since they were people with close family ties and weekly parties, they suddenly understood the situation. I was a poor little girl who was caring for my drunken father, who had stayed too long at the party.

The guard began waking Dad. When he woke up, he asked, "*¿Qué pasa? ¿Qué quiere?*" Anyone else would have asked, "Where am I?" Obviously, this was a common Mexican experience. When I knew that he could understand I went to the car, calmly pushed the people away, and said, "Dad, there's been an accident." He recognized me slowly and became my pre-Mexican-party father.

"An accident?" he asked. "Whose fault was it? Yours, Marguerite? Was it your fault?"

"Yes, Dad, I drove into a car."

"In the box. The insurance papers. Get them, give them to the police, and then come back."

The guard asked Dad to get out of the car. My father reached in the box and took out the folded papers and the half bottle of alcohol he had left there earlier. He laughed, got out of the car, and put his arm around the other driver's shoulder. He spoke to the guard, and the three men walked into the kiosk. Within minutes, laughter burst from the kiosk and the crisis was over. But so was the enjoyment.

Dad shook hands with all the men, patted the children, and smiled at the women. Then, and without looking at the damaged cars, he sat in the driver's seat and called me to get in. As if he had not been helplessly drunk a half hour earlier, he drove home. He said he didn't know I could drive, and how did I like his car? I was angry that he had recovered so quickly and disappointed that he didn't appreciate the greatness of my achievement. So I answered "yes" to both the statement and the question. Before we reached the border he rolled down the window, and the fresh air was uncomfortably cold. We drove into the city in a cold private silence.

Dolores was sitting, it seemed, in the same place as the night before. Dad said, "Hello, kid," and walked toward the bathroom. I greeted her, "Hello, Dolores," and went to my room. Within minutes an argument began in the living room.

"Bailey, you've let your children come between us."

"Kid, you're too sensitive. The children—my children—can't come between us, unless you let them."

"How can I stop it?" She was crying. "Bailey, you know I wanted to like your children, but they . . ." She couldn't make herself describe us. "I'm marrying you. I don't want to marry your children."

82

"That's your problem, woman. I'm going out. Goodnight."

The front door shut loudly. Dolores cried quietly.

In my room, I thought my father was mean and cruel. He had enjoyed his Mexican holiday, and still was unable to offer a bit of kindness to the woman who had waited patiently. I felt sorry and even a little guilty. I had enjoyed myself, too. There was nothing fair or kind about the way my father treated her, so I decided to go out and comfort her. I stood in the center of the floor but Dolores never even looked up. I said in my nicest voice, "Dolores, I don't mean to come between you and Dad. I wish you'd believe me."

With her head still bent down she said, "No one was speaking to you, Marguerite. It's rude to listen to other people's conversations."

"I wasn't listening. These walls are so thin a deaf person could have heard what you said. I thought I'd tell you that I have no interest in coming between you and my father. That's all." I turned to go.

"No, that's not all." She looked up. "Why don't you go back to your mother? If you've got one."

"I've got one, and she's much better than you, prettier, too, and intelligent and—"

"And"—her voice reached a high point—"she's a prostitute." The awful accusation struck not so much at my daughterly love as at the basis of my new existence. If there was a chance that it was true, I would not be able to live, to continue to live with Mother. And I wanted to very much.

Angry, I walked over to Dolores and hit her. She jumped out of her chair, and before I could jump back, she had her arms around me. Neither of us made a sound until I finally pushed her back on to the sofa. Then she started screaming.

I walked out of the house. On the steps I felt something wet on my arm, looked down, and found blood. I was cut. Dolores opened the door, screaming still, and ran like a crazy woman down the stairs. I saw a hammer in her hand and ran. I jumped in Dad's car, rolled up the windows, and locked the door. Dolores ran around the car, screaming like a crazy person.

Daddy Bailey and the neighbors he was visiting responded to the screams and crowded around her. My father motioned to me to open the window. When I did, he said that he would take Dolores inside but I should stay in the car. He would be back to take care of me.

My father came down the steps in a few minutes and angrily got in the car. He sat in a corner of blood and felt the dampness on his pants.

"What the hell is this?" he asked.

I said calmly, "I've been cut."

"When? By whom?"

"Dolores cut me."

"How badly?" he asked.

"I don't know."

He started the car and took me to his friends' house. I followed the woman to a bedroom, and she asked me where I was hurt. I pulled off my dress and we both looked at the wound on my side, which had begun to heal. She washed it with medicine and put a bandage on it. Then we went into the living room. Dad shook hands with the man he'd been talking to, thanked my emergency nurse, and we left.

In the car he explained that he had telephoned other friends and made arrangements for me to spend the night with them. At another strange house I was taken in and given night clothes and a bed. Dad said he'd see me at noon the next day.

In the morning I made and ate a big breakfast and sat down with a magazine to wait for Dad. At fifteen, life had taught me that surrender, sometimes, was as honorable as resistance, especially if one had no choice. When my father came, he asked how I felt, gave me a dollar and a half and a kiss, and said he'd return late in the evening. He laughed as usual. Was he nervous?

Alone, I imagined the owners returning to find me in their house, and realized that I didn't even remember what they looked like. How could I accept their pity? If I disappeared Dad would be glad; Dolores would be happy, too. What would I do? Then I thought of Bailey. What would he do? He ordered me to leave.

I made a few sandwiches, put a bandage supply in my pocket, counted my money (I had over three dollars plus some Mexican coins), and walked out. When I heard the door close, I knew my decision was final. I didn't have a key and nothing would make me stand around until Dad's friends returned to pityingly let me back in.

I was free, and I started thinking about my future. The obvious solution to my homelessness concerned me only briefly. I could go home to Mother, but I couldn't. I could never succeed in hiding the cut in my side from her. And if I failed to hide the wound we were certain to experience another scene of violence. I thought of poor Mr. Freeman, and the guilt which remained in my heart, even after all those years, returned.

I spent the day wandering through the streets. I went to the library and used part of my day reading. I used its washroom to change my bandage.

On one street I passed a yard filled with old abandoned cars. As I walked through them, a temporary solution came to mind. I would find a clean car and spend the night in it. In my optimistic ignorance I thought that I'd think of a more pleasant solution in the morning. The idea of sleeping outdoors strengthened my sense of freedom. After deciding on a car, I got inside and ate the sandwiches. I decided to sit there and wait for sleep.

The morning's brightness awoke me and I was surrounded with strangeness. When I sat up, I saw a mixture of Negro,

Mexican, and white faces outside the windows. They were laughing. They looked so curious that I knew they wouldn't go away before they knew who I was, so I opened the door and got out. I was asked my name, where I came from, and what led me to the abandoned cars. They accepted my explanation that I was from San Francisco, that my name was Marguerite but that I was called Maya, and that I had no place to stay. They welcomed me and said I could stay as long as I honored their rule: No two people of opposite sex slept together. In fact everyone had his own private sleeping place. There was no stealing because a crime would bring the police. Everyone worked at something, and all the money was shared by the whole community.

During the month I spent there, my thinking processes changed so I hardly recognized myself. My old insecurity was gone as a result of the unquestioning acceptance by the others. After looking for unbroken bottles and selling them with a white girl from Missouri, a Mexican girl from Los Angeles, and a Black girl from Oklahoma, I never again felt so completely separated from the rest of society. The lack of criticism in our community influenced me, and made me tolerant for life.

I telephoned Mother (her voice reminded me of another world) and asked her to send for me. When she said she was going to send my air ticket to Daddy, I explained that it would be easier if she sent the fare to the airline, then I'd pick it up. She agreed. After I picked up my ticket I announced rather casually that I would be leaving the following day. Everyone wished me well.

I arrived in San Francisco, thinner than usual, dirty, and with no luggage. Mother took one look and said, "Isn't there enough to eat at your father's? You'd better have some food to stick to those bones."

I was home, again. And my mother was a fine lady. Dolores was a fool and, more important, a liar.

Chapter 14 San Francisco

The house seemed smaller and quieter after the trip south, and San Francisco didn't seem as exciting. I realized that I had given up some youth for knowledge, but my gain was more valuable than the loss.

Bailey was much older, too. Even years older than I had become. He had made new friends and his language had changed. He may have been glad to see me, but he didn't act like it. When I tried to tell him of my adventures, he responded with a lack of interest which stopped my stories. His new companions drank alcohol secretly and told bad jokes. Although I had no regrets, I told myself sadly that growing up was not the painless process one expected it to be.

In one area my brother and I found ourselves closer. I had learned public dancing, and Mother allowed us to go to the big band dances in the city hall. In a few months handsome Bailey and his tall sister were famous.

Although I had risked my life (not intentionally) in her defense, Mother's reputation, good name, and community image ceased being of interest to me. I didn't care for her less, but I was less concerned about everything and everyone. I often thought how boring life was after one had seen all its surprises. In two months, I had become uninterested.

♦

Mother and Bailey were having mother–son problems. Bailey was sixteen and hopelessly in love with Mother Dear. Her heroes and her friends were rich gamblers who wore expensive clothes. How could a sixteen-year-old boy hope to compete with such rivals? He did what he had to do. He acquired a white prostitute, a diamond ring on his finger, and an expensive jacket. He didn't consciously think of the new possessions as a way to gain Mother

Dear's acceptance. And she had no idea that her preferences led him to such excesses.

From another room I heard their arguments and listened hopelessly. I was left out of their power–love struggles.

One night he came home at one o'clock, two hours late.

"I guess you're a man . . ." she said to him.

"I'm your son, Mother Dear," he responded.

"Clidell is the only man in this house, and if you think you're so much of a man . . ." Her voice was angry.

"I'm leaving now, Mother Dear," he announced.

"Then get moving." And Bailey went to his room.

Bailey was leaving home. At one o'clock in the morning my brother, who had always protected me, was leaving home. I went to his room and found him throwing his clothes into a pillowcase. His maturity embarrassed me. He didn't look like my brother. Not knowing what to say, I asked if I could help, and he answered, "Leave me alone."

I leaned on the door, giving him my physical presence, but said no more.

"She wants me out, does she?" he continued, talking to himself. "Well, I'll get out of here fast. She won't see me here again. I'll be OK. I'll always be OK."

At some point he noticed me in the doorway. "Maya, if you want to leave now, come on. I'll take care of you."

He didn't wait for an answer, but quickly returned to speaking to his soul. "She won't miss me, and I won't miss her. To hell with her and everybody else."

He had finished pushing his shoes on top of his shirts and ties and socks in the pillowcase. He remembered me again.

"Maya, you can have my books," he said. Then he grabbed the pillowcase, pushed past me, and headed for the stairs. I heard the front door shut loudly.

Mother's eyes were red the next morning, but she smiled. No

one mentioned Bailey's absence, as if things were as they should be and always were.

I believed I knew where he had gone the night before, and decided to try to find him and offer him my support. In the afternoon I went to the house. A woman answered the doorbell and said Bailey Johnson was at the top of the stairs. His eyes were as red as Mother's had been, but his face was not as angry as it had been the night before. I was invited in.

He began to talk about everything except our unusual situation. Eventually he said, "Maya, you know, it's better this way . . . I mean, I'm a man, and I have to be on my own . . ."

I was angry that he didn't curse Mother or at least act upset.

"This morning Mother Dear came here. We had a very good discussion." He chose his words carefully. "She understands completely. There's a time in every man's life when he must leave the safety of home and go out on his own. She's arranging with a friend of hers to get me a job on the trains. I'll learn the job and then get a better one. The future looks good."

If I'd had any suggestions to make, he wouldn't have heard them. And, most regrettable, I had no suggestion to make.

"I'm your sister, and I'll do whatever I can," I told him.

"Maya, don't worry about me. That's all I want you to do. Don't worry. I'll be OK."

I left his room because, and only because, we had said all we could say. The unsaid words made us feel uncomfortable.

Back in my room, I felt depressed. It was going to be impossible for me to stay there. Running away from home wouldn't be right, either. But I needed a change.

I would go to work. It would be easy to persuade Mother. I was a year ahead of my grade in school and Mother believed in taking care of oneself. After I had made that decision, I just needed to decide which kind of job I was most suited to. Because of the war, women had replaced men as conductors on the streetcars, and the thought of riding up and down the hills of San Francisco in a dark-blue uniform, with a money changer on my belt, was appealing. When Mother asked what I planned to do, I replied that I would get a job on the streetcars. She rejected the idea with: "They don't accept colored people on the streetcars."

My first reaction was disappointment. I'd pictured myself dressed in a neat, blue suit, my money changer swinging at my waist, with a cheerful smile for the passengers which would make their own work day brighter. I told her again that I would go to work on the streetcars and wear a blue suit, and she gave me her support. "That's what you want to do? Nothing beats trying except failure. Give it your best effort."

It was the most positive encouragement I could have hoped for.

♦

In the offices of the Market Street Railway Company, the receptionist seemed surprised to see me there. I explained that I had come to ask about a job. She asked if I was sent by an agency, and when I replied that I was not, she told me that they were only accepting applicants from agencies.

"I'm applying for the job listed in this morning's *Chronicle* and I'd like to be presented to your personnel manager."

"He's out for the day. You could come back tomorrow and if he's in, I'm sure you can see him." Then she turned her chair around and I was supposed to be dismissed.

"May I ask his name?"

She half turned, acting surprised to find me still there.

"His name? Whose name?"

"The personnel manager."

"The personnel manager? Oh, he's Mr. Cooper, but I'm not sure you'll find him here tomorrow. He's . . . but you can try."

"Thank you."

"You're welcome."

And I was out of the room and out of the building. I thought about our conversation. It wasn't personal. The incident was a repeating dream, made up years before by stupid whites, and it always returned. I accepted the receptionist as another victim of the rules of society.

On the streetcar, I put my fare into the box and the conductor looked at me with the usual hard eyes of white contempt. "Move into the car, please move on in the car." She patted her money changer.

Her Southern accent interrupted my thoughts. All lies, all comfortable lies. The receptionist was not innocent and neither was I. The whole situation in that waiting room was directly about me, Black, and her, white.

I wouldn't move into the streetcar but stood on the platform. My mind shouted.

I WOULD HAVE THE JOB. I WOULD BE A CONDUCTOR AND HANG A MONEY CHANGER FROM MY BELT. I WOULD.

I was determined. During the next three weeks the Negro organizations to whom I appealed for support sent me from one to another. Why did I insist on that particular job? There were opportunities that paid almost twice the money. They thought I was crazy. Possibly I was.

During this period of strain, Mother and I began our first steps on the long path toward shared adult admiration. She never asked for reports and I didn't offer any details. But every morning she made breakfast, and gave me carfare and lunch money, as if I were going to work. She understood that I had to try every possibility before giving up.

On my way out of the house one morning she said, "Life is going to give you what you put in it. Put your whole heart in everything you do, and pray, then you can wait." Another time she reminded me that "God helps those who help themselves." Strangely, as bored as I was with these sayings, her way of saying them gave them something new, and started me thinking—for a little while at least. Later, when she asked how I got my job, I was never able to say exactly. I only knew that one day I sat in the railway office, pretending to be waiting to be interviewed. The receptionist called me to her desk and pushed a bundle of papers to me. They were the application forms. I had little time to wonder if I had won or not, because the standard questions reminded me of the necessity for lying. How old was I? List my previous jobs. How much money did I earn, and why did I leave the position? Give two references (not relatives).

Sitting at a side table, I made a story of near-truths and total lies. I kept my face without expression and wrote quickly the story of Marguerite Johnson, age nineteen, former companion and driver for Mrs. Annie Henderson (a white lady) in Stamps, Arkansas.

I was given a number of tests. Then on one happy day I was hired as the first Negro on the San Francisco streetcars.

Mother gave me the money to have my blue suit made, and I learned to fill out work cards and operate the money changer. Soon I was standing on the back of the streetcar, smiling sweetly and persuading my passengers to "step forward in the car, please."

For one whole semester the streetcars and I went up and down the hills of San Francisco. My work shifts were split so much that it was easy to believe my superiors had chosen them with bad intentions. When I mentioned my suspicions to Mother, she said, "Don't worry about it. You ask for what you want, and you pay for what you get."

She stayed awake to drive me out to the streetcar garage at four-thirty in the mornings, or to pick me up when I was finished just before dawn. She knew that I was safe on the public transportation, but she wouldn't trust a taxi driver with her baby.

When spring classes began, I returned to my commitment to formal education. I was much wiser and older, much more independent, with a bank account and clothes that I had bought for myself. I was sure that I had learned and earned what was necessary to be a part of the life of my classmates.

Within weeks, however, I realized that my schoolmates and I were on opposite paths. They were concerned and excited over football games, but I had recently raced a car down a dark and foreign Mexican mountain. They concentrated their interest on who would be the school president, and when the metal bands would be removed from their teeth, while I remembered sleeping for a month in an abandoned car and working in a streetcar in the early hours of the morning. I realized that the things I still had to learn wouldn't be taught to me at George Washington High School.

I began missing classes, walking in Golden Gate Park, or wandering in the department store. When Mother discovered that I wasn't going to school, she told me that if I didn't want to go to school one day, I should tell her, and I could stay home. She said that she didn't want a white woman calling her to tell her something about her child that she didn't know. She didn't want to have to lie to a white woman because I wasn't woman enough to talk to her. That ended my days of not going to school, but nothing changed to make it a better place for me to be.

Chapter 15   Maturity

I was fascinated by lesbians and I feared that I was one. I noticed how deep my voice had become. It was lower than my schoolmates' voices. My hands and feet were not feminine and small. In front of the mirror I examined my body. For a sixteen-year-old my breasts were sadly underdeveloped. The skin under my arms was as smooth as my face. I began to wonder: How did lesbianism begin? What were the signs of it?

One night a classmate of mine called to ask if she could sleep at my house. My mother gave permission. In my room we shared mean gossip about our friends, giggled about boys, and complained about school and life. Since my friend had nothing to sleep in, I gave her one of my nightdresses, and without curiosity or interest I watched her pull off her clothes. I wasn't conscious of her body. Then suddenly, for a brief moment, I saw her breasts. I was shocked. They were small, but they were real. They were beautiful. A universe divided what she had from what I had. She was a woman.

If I'd been older I might have thought that I was excited by both a sense of beauty and the emotion of envy. But those possibilities did not occur to me then. All I knew was that I had been excited by looking at a woman's breasts. Something about me wasn't normal. I was miserable. I must be a lesbian. After examining myself, I reasoned that I didn't have any of the obvious characteristics—I didn't wear pants, or have big shoulders, or walk like a man, or even want to touch a woman. I wanted to be a woman, but that seemed to be a world which I was not going to be allowed to enter.

What I needed was a boyfriend. A boyfriend's acceptance of me would guide me into femininity. Among the people I knew, no one was interested. Understandably the boys of my age and social group were interested in the yellow- or light-brown-skinned girls, with hairy legs, smooth little lips, and long straight hair. What could an unattractive female do?

I decided I had to do something. Two handsome brothers lived up the hill from our house. If I was going to try to have sex, I saw no reason why I shouldn't experiment with the best candidates. I didn't expect to interest either brother permanently, but I thought I could interest one temporarily.

I made a plan that started with surprise. One evening as I

walked up the hill, the brother I had chosen came walking directly into my trap.

"Hello, Marguerite." He nearly passed me.

I put the plan into action. "Hey," I began, "would you like to have sex with me?" His mouth hung open. I had the advantage and so I used it.

"Take me somewhere."

He asked, "You mean you're going to let me have sex with you?"

I assured him that that was exactly what I was going to do. He thought I was giving him something, but the fact was that it was my intention to take something from him. His good looks and popularity had made him so proud that he couldn't see that possibility.

We went to a furnished room occupied by one of his friends, who understood the situation immediately, got his coat, and left us alone. He immediately turned off the lights. I was excited rather than nervous, and hopeful instead of frightened. I had not considered how physical the act would be. I had anticipated long kisses and gentle touches. But there was nothing romantic about the knee which forced my legs open, nor in the rub of hairy skin on my chest.

Not one word was spoken.

My partner showed that our experience had ended by getting up suddenly, and my main concern was how to get home quickly. He may have sensed that he had been used, or his lack of interest may have been an indication that I was less than satisfying. Neither possibility bothered me.

Outside on the street we left each other with little more than "OK, see you around."

Thanks to Mr. Freeman nine years before, I had had no pain of entry, and because of the absence of romantic involvement, neither of us felt that much had happened.

At home I reviewed the failure and considered my new position. I had had a man. I had been had. I not only didn't enjoy it, but whether I was normal or not was still a question.

There seemed to be no explanation for my private problem, but being a product ("victim" may be a better word) of the Southern Negro values, I decided that I "would understand it all better later." I went to sleep.

Three weeks later, having thought very little about the strange night, I realized that I was pregnant.

♦

The world had ended, and I was the only person who knew it. If I could have a baby I obviously wasn't a lesbian, but the little pleasure I was able to take from that fact was overcome by fear, guilt, and self-contempt. I had to accept that I had brought this disaster on myself. How could I blame the innocent man whom I had asked to make love to me?

I finally sent a letter to Bailey, who was at sea with the navy. He wrote back, and he warned me against telling Mother of my condition. We both knew she would very likely order me to leave school. Bailey suggested that if I left school before getting my high school diploma I'd find it almost impossible to return.

During the first three months, while I was adapting myself to the fact of pregnancy (I didn't link pregnancy to the possibility of having a baby until weeks before its end) the days seemed to mix together. The passing of time was never completely clear.

Fortunately, Mother was busy with her own life. As long as I was healthy, clothed, and smiling, she felt no need to concentrate her attention on me. As always, her major concern was to live the life given to her, and her children were expected to do the same. And to do it without being too much bother.

My breasts grew larger, and my brown skin grew smooth and tight. And still she didn't suspect. Years before, I had developed a behavior which never varied. I didn't lie. It was understood that I didn't lie because I was too proud to be caught and forced to admit that I was capable of lying. Mother must have decided that since I didn't lie I also didn't deceive. She was deceived.

All my motions were concentrated on pretending to be the innocent schoolgirl who had nothing to worry about except exams. School recovered its lost magic. For the first time since Stamps, information was exciting for itself. I buried myself in facts, and found delight in the logic of mathematics.

Halfway through my pregnancy, Bailey came home. As my sixth month approached, Mother left San Francisco for Alaska. She was going to open a nightclub and planned to stay three or four months. Daddy Clidell was told to look after me but I was more or less left on my own.

Mother left the city with a cheerful send-off party, and I felt deceitful for allowing her to go without informing her that she would soon be a grandmother.

◆

Two days after the war ended, I stood with the San Francisco Summer School class at Mission High School and received my diploma. That evening I revealed my fearful secret and, in a brave gesture, left a note on Daddy Clidell's bed. It read: *Dear Parents, I am sorry to bring this disgrace on the family, but I am pregnant. Marguerite.*

The confusion that followed when I explained to Daddy Clidell that I expected to deliver the baby in about three weeks wasn't funny until years later. He told Mother that I was "three weeks along." Mother, back from Alaska and regarding me as a woman for the first time, said, "She's more than three weeks." They both accepted the fact that I had been pregnant longer than they had first been told, but it was impossible for them to believe that I had carried a baby for eight months and one week, without their noticing.

97

Mother asked, "Who's the boy?" I told her.

"Do you want to marry him?"

"No."

"Does he want to marry you?" The father had stopped speaking to me during my fourth month.

"No."

"Well, that's that. No use in ruining three lives." There was no criticism. She was Vivian Baxter Jackson. Hoping for the best, prepared for the worst, and unsurprised by anything in between.

Daddy Clidell assured me that I had nothing to worry about. He sent one of his waitresses to buy dresses for me. For the next two weeks I went to doctors, bought clothes for the baby, and enjoyed the coming event.

Quickly and without too much pain, my son was born. In my mind gratefulness was confused with love, and possession became mixed up with motherhood. I had a baby. He was beautiful and mine. Totally mine. No one had bought him for me. No one had helped me through the months of pregnancy.

I was afraid to touch him. Home from the hospital, I sat for hours by his bed and admired his mysterious perfection. Mother handled him easily and with confidence, but I feared being forced to hold him. Wasn't I famous for awkwardness? I was afraid I might drop him.

Mother came to my bed one night bringing my three-week-old baby. She explained that he was going to sleep with me.

I begged uselessly. I was sure to roll over and crush out his life or break his bones. She wouldn't listen, and within minutes the pretty golden baby was lying on his back in the center of my bed, laughing at me.

I lay on the edge of the bed, stiff with fear, and promised not to sleep all night long. But I fell asleep.

My shoulder was shaken gently. Mother whispered, "Maya, wake up. But don't move."

I knew immediately that the awakening was about the baby. I became tense. "I'm awake."

She turned the light on and said, "Look at the baby." My fears were so powerful that I couldn't move to look at the center of the bed. She said again, "Look at the baby." I didn't hear sadness in her voice, and that helped me stop being frightened. The baby was no longer in the center of the bed. At first I thought he had moved. But after closer investigation, I found that I was lying on my stomach with my arm bent at a right angle. Under the tent of blanket, formed by my elbow and arm, the baby slept touching my side.

Mother whispered, "See, you don't have to think about doing the right thing. If you're for the right thing, then you do it without thinking."

She turned out the light, and I patted my son's body lightly and went back to sleep.

ACTIVITIES

Chapters 1–3

Before you read

1 What do you think it was like growing up as a Black child in the Southern part of the U. S. in the 1930s and 1940s?

2 Find these words in your dictionary. They are all used in this book.

ain't   conductor   cripple   hostility   pee   pineapple

Which:

  a is a food?

  b describes a person who is disabled?

  c is a word not used in standard English?

  d is usually done in a toilet?

  e describes a person's feelings toward an enemy?

  f is a person who works on a train or streetcar?

3 Answer the questions. Find the words in *italics* in your dictionary.

  a What *chores* do you do at home?

  b What would bring *disgrace* to you or your family?

  c Is your hair *kinky*? What's it like?

  d Is your city/town *segregated*? If so, explain how.

  e Do you know anyone who *stutters*? How do they feel about it?

After you read

4 Who is described by the following statements? What is their importance to Maya?

  a "He was proud and sensitive."

  b "the greatest person in my world"

  c "His attitude was meant to show his authority and power."

  d "an independent Black man"

5 Discuss these questions.

  a Why do you think Maya didn't believe that white people were real?

  b Do you think Stamps was a good place to grow up? Why (not)?

Chapters 4–6

Before you read

6 In Chapter 5, Maya moves away from Stamps and gets a new family. How do you think she will feel?

7 Find these words in your dictionary. Use them to complete the phrases below.

   apron   contempt   doll   ignorance   handstand   impudent
   lot   mate

   a treat someone with .....
   b be ..... to someone
   c give a child a .....
   d wear an .....
   e invite your .....
   f show your ..... of the facts
   g do a .....
   h the parking .....

8 Answer the questions. Find the words in *italics* in your dictionary.

   a Have you ever experienced *prejudice*? If so, explain the situation and your reaction.
   b What is the punishment for *rape* in your country?

After you read

9 Choose one of these people and prepare a short talk. Say what you know about them, how Maya feels about them, and what you think of their personality and behavior.

   a Momma   **c** Mother
   b Maya's father **d** Mr. Freeman

10 Who do you think killed Mr. Freeman? Why? What do you think would have happened if he had not been killed?

Chapters 7–9

Before you read

11 Why do you think Maya returns to Stamps? How do you think she feels about being back in Stamps? What do you think her life will be like there now?

12 Find these words in your dictionary. Use them to complete the sentences.

errand   giggle   valentine

a Girls often ..... with their friends over silly things.

b The boy helps his mother by doing ..... for her.

c Children exchange ..... with their classmates.

After you read

13 Why are the following important to Maya? What effect do they have on her life?

a cookies   **d** a picnic

b dishes   **e** a valentine

c a movie

14 Discuss these questions.

a Maya says, "After being a woman for three years I became a girl." What do you think she means?

b Miss Glory tells Maya, "Sticks and stones may break your bones, but words will never hurt you." Do you agree or disagree? Explain.

c Do you think using a person's name correctly is important? Why (not)?

Chapters 10–12

Before you read

15 Why do you think Maya goes to California?

16 Find these words in your dictionary. Match each with a word below. Explain the connection.

anthem   con   mature   semester

a adult   **b** school   **c** trick   **d** song

After you read

17 Work in pairs. Role-play this imaginary conversation.

Student A: You are Maya. You have just listened to Mr. Donleavy's remarks at your graduation. You are angry.

Student B: You are Mr. Donleavy. You are in a hurry and don't really want to talk to this girl. You think she is impudent.

18 Why do you think Maya feels safer in San Francisco than in other places she has lived?

Chapters 13–15

Before you read

19 What do you think Maya's life is like when she is sixteen? What is she doing? How does she feel about her life?

20 Find these words in your dictionary. Which is a word for a job?
lesbian   prostitute

After you read

21 Discuss these questions.
   a How do you explain the differences in Daddy Bailey's behavior in Stamps, Los Angeles, and Mexico?
   b How has Maya's relationship with her mother changed?
   c After reading about her life, why do you think Ms. Angelou chose the title *I Know Why the Caged Bird Sings* for the first part of her life story?

Writing

22 Choose three adjectives to describe Momma. Explain your choices.

23 Imagine that you are Maya as a young adult. Write a letter to Mother about Mr. Freeman and his effect on your life.

24 The Store was Maya's favorite place as a young child. Describe your favorite place during your childhood. Why was it important to you?

25 Compare Maya's life in Stamps, St. Louis, and San Francisco. Which place do you think was the best place for a Black girl to live? Why?

26 In her childhood, Maya was strongly influenced by Mrs. Flowers, the woman in Stamps who gave her books, and Miss Kirwin, the only teacher she can still remember. Describe two people who were important in your life as you grew up. How did they influence you?

27 Compare Maya's life from age 3 to 16 with your life between those ages. What are the main similarities and differences?

BESTSELLING
PENGUIN READERS

AT LEVEL 6

Brave New World

The Chamber

Cry, the Beloved Country

Great Expectations

Kolymsky Heights

Memoirs of a Geisha

Misery

Oliver Twist

Presumed Innocent

The Remains of the Day

Saving Private Ryan

Snow Falling on Cedars